VISITORS' HISTORIC BRITAIN

CORNWALL

ROMANS TO VICTORIANS

VISITORS' HISTORIC BRITAIN

CORNWALL

ROMANS TO VICTORIANS

DEREK TAIT

PEN & SWORD
HISTORY

First published in Great Britain in 2018 by
Pen & Sword History
An imprint of
Pen & Sword Books Ltd
Yorkshire – Philadelphia

ISBN 978 1 52672 170 9

Printed and bound in England
By CPI Group (UK) Ltd, Croydon, CR0 4YY
Typeset by Aura Technology and Software Services, India

Pen & Sword Books Limited incorporates the imprints of Atlas, Archaeology, Aviation,
Discovery, Family History, Fiction, History, Maritime, Military, Military Classics,
Politics, Select, Transport, True Crime, Air World, Frontline Publishing, Leo Cooper,
Remember When, Seaforth Publishing, The Praetorian Press, Wharncliffe Local
History, Wharncliffe Transport, Wharncliffe True Crime and White Owl.

For a complete list of Pen & Sword titles please contact

PEN & SWORD BOOKS LIMITED
47 Church Street, Barnsley, South Yorkshire, S70 2AS, England
E-mail: enquiries@pen-and-sword.co.uk
Website: www.pen-and-sword.co.uk

Or
PEN AND SWORD BOOKS
1950 Lawrence Rd, Havertown, PA 19083, USA
E-mail: Uspen-and-sword@casematepublishers.com
Website: www.penandswordbooks.com

Contents

Introduction

Cornwall is one of the most historic and beautiful counties in Great Britain. With its amazing scenery, stretching from Saltash to Land's End, it features some of the best and most interesting places to visit in the country.

The area was first inhabited during the Palaeolithic and Mesolithic periods and continued to be occupied during the Neolithic and Bronze Age periods as many relics from this time have been discovered. Although Roman rule was thought not to have stretched west of Exeter, artefacts of Romans living in the area have been found including coins, pottery and a gold pestle on the Rame Peninsula. For more recent times, scattered across the county are many picturesque abandoned tin mines as well as other relics of Cornwall's past.

Tourism plays a large part in the prosperity of Cornwall today and the once thriving industries such as fishing, mining and agriculture have now long gone or are greatly diminished. When the railway was introduced and the Royal Albert Bridge was built by Brunel, spanning the River Tamar in the 1800s, Cornwall became more accessible and a popular destination for day trippers and holidaymakers during the Victorian and Edwardian periods. Hotels were built in the early nineteenth century and catered for the many tourists who visited the county. Many of these original buildings still exist, although some have seen better days. With the rise in popularity of the seaside holiday, Cornwall came alive with visitors; cafés and tearooms opened up to greet the surge of people, some of whom hadn't seen the sea before.

Much has changed all over the county. Some Victorian holiday resorts have become very run down and today look worse for wear.

Cornwall is said to be one of the poorest counties in Britain. However, it is still a popular holiday destination and is also enjoyed by surfers and other water sport enthusiasts. Regular surfing championship events take place in Newquay and annual sailing events and regattas are held in the many ports around the region, including Falmouth and Fowey.

In recent years, attractions like the Eden Project and the Tate Gallery in St Ives have attracted hundreds of thousands of visitors. Rick Stein's restaurants in Padstow have also greatly revived the area.

Second homes have resulted in many small villages and towns appearing empty out of season. Fishing villages, once full of Cornishmen and their families, are now a thing of the past.

This book looks at Cornwall's rich and diverse history and tells stories of prehistoric times, the legend of King Arthur, the days of tin mining and prosperous fishing industries, the English Civil War and much more, teaching the visitor all there is to know about the hidden history of the county.

CHAPTER 1

Saltash to Fowey

Saltash is the first place arrived at in Cornwall after crossing the Tamar by either the Tamar Bridge or the Royal Albert Bridge from Devon.

The area was originally called 'Ash' which referred to the many Ash trees that once grew there. The Middle English version of the name Ash was 'Esse'. The area fell within the manor of Trematon and, when a member of the de Valletort family, who were the Lords of Trematon, built streets on the adjoining hillside in 1175, the waterside area was absorbed into the new borough. The market town flourished and became an important port. Other places in the South West were called Ash, so the town was prefixed with the word, 'Salt' to distinguish itself from the other communities in about 1300.

Although outgrown by Plymouth in the 1300s, Saltash continued to prosper and, with its deep-water anchorage, it was able to accommodate ships of all sizes. A small fleet of ships, crewed by local men, were kept by Saltash merchants. These ships were requisitioned for various war service over the centuries. There is a Saltash saying, 'Saltash was a borough town when Plymouth was a fuzzy down', which refers to Plymouth not being a seaport when Saltash was already established. Flint arrowheads and skin scrapers dating back from 4,000 to 1,500BC have been found in the fields around Saltash. There was also possibly a Roman settlement on the Saltash side of the ferry crossing.

In the seventh century, Trematon was the Celtic capital and in the ninth century, Anglo Saxons inhabited the area. Saxon rule ended with the Norman conquest of 1066 when Brian of Brittany became the Lord of the Manor. In 1068 William the Conqueror ordered that castles be built in the south-west after a rebellion. One of these castles was built at Trematon and was to become the overseer of the community. Robert, Count of Mortain (William's half brother) was put in charge of Trematon and soon after founded a market. In 1075, Richard de Valletort, a knight who had fought at the Battle of Hastings, took control of Trematon from Robert and he founded a borough close to the castle. He also had built the parish church of St Stephen.

During Henry II's reign a port was built at Saltash for the export of tin from local mines. In 1190 a new borough was set up by the de Valletorts near the Tamar foreshore. During this time, the market thrived, as did other activities based around the waterfront, including boat building, fishing and the ferry. This ran between Devon and Cornwall for hundreds of years and was the main route between the two counties before the building of the Royal Albert Bridge in 1859.

The de Valletort family owned the rights to the ferry from the Norman Conquest until 1270. From 1337 the ferry was leased for £10 a year to the Duchy of Cornwall. They continued to hold the lease each year apart from 1357 when it was leased to William Lenche who was the Black Prince's military porter. This was seen as a reward for Lenche's service at the Battle of Poitiers, a war fought in 1356 between the English and the French.

The Mayor and Burgesses of Saltash were granted the rights to the ferry in 1385. These rights lasted 200 years and the rent was paid directly to the Duchy of Cornwall. In 1733 the ferry overturned and sank with a loss of twenty lives.

There have been seven ferries since the introduction of the Saltash Floating Bridge Act of 1832 which allowed the Earl of Morley, Sir William Molesworth, Mr A. Edgcumbe and others to purchase the ferry rights and to establish a steam powered ferry. The ferry continued to run until its last journey on 21 October 1961 when the Tamar Bridge opened.

An early scene of the beach at Saltash. During Henry II's reign, a port was set up at Saltash for the export of tin from local mines. In 1190 a new borough was set up by the de Valletorts near the Tamar foreshore.

Saltash grew up around the area of the waterfront where the ferry service was in operation for hundreds of years. The site of Tamar Street was once home to both fishermen and ferrymen. The area around the water's edge has changed dramatically over the last 100 years. Once thriving with fishermen and cockle sellers, in 1957 the whole area, much to the dismay of its residents, was declared a slum and it was decided that many of the buildings should be demolished. This was a great shame as some buildings dated back to the 1500s and were as Sir Francis Drake, and many of his compatriots, would have once seen them. Clearing the area, ripped away much of Saltash's history. At the time, the old industrial buildings were also removed, along with the gasworks which had closed in 1947. Buildings associated with fishing and boat building also disappeared. The three public houses remained although part of the Passage Inn (later renamed the Boatman) was demolished. A small, then modern, housing estate appeared in its place.

Several famous people have had connections with the town including the Hawkins family and of course, Mary Newman, the wife of Francis Drake, who was said to have lived at Culver Road.

When Drake landed at Saltash in 1587, the people helped unload the captured Portuguese ship, *San Felipe*. Drake had taken the ship on his way back home from a successful attack on the Spanish fleet. The cargo contained jewels, gold and spices which would be worth around the equivalent of £12 million today. The people of Saltash had never seen such treasure. Over £6,000 worth of spices were sold in Saltash while the rest of the treasure was taken back to London to be presented to Queen Elizabeth I. Moored in the River Tamar, the *San Felipe* caught fire and was destroyed. Parts of the ship were discovered in 1902 when dredging work was carried out.

The ship *John Trelawney* was equipped by the people of Saltash and proved successful in seeing off the Spanish Armada in 1588.

The property in Culver Road has been known as Mary Newman's Cottage for many years, but many would dispute that she ever lived there. The cottage itself dates from 1480 and Mary was said to have been born there. It has been suggested that Mary was actually from St Budeaux and that her father was Henry Newman and records of the marriages of his five children, including Mary, are recorded at the church at Higher St Budeaux. Plymouth also lays claim to being Mary's birthplace and local legend suggests that she was actually born at Agaton Farm and possibly lived, at some time, in the barn that still stands off Normandy Hill. The Newman family were important members of the community. Little is known about Mary Newman, no paintings or drawings exist, and details of her life are sketchy.

What is known, is that she married Francis Drake, then a young sailor, in 1569. They were married for 12 years until Mary died in 1581. Her cause of death is unknown though some suggest that she died of smallpox. Her grave lies where she was married, at the church at Higher St Budeaux in Plymouth although its location has been lost over the years.

While they were married, Francis Drake spent much of his time at sea. During this time, he became wealthy, famous and was knighted by Queen Elizabeth I. Drake was married again in 1585 to Elizabeth Sydenham and they moved to Buckland Abbey. They had no children.

During the English Civil War between 1642 and 1646, it is said that more Roundheads (Parliamentarians) died in the River Tamar from drowning after taking flight from the Battle of Braddock Down than those who died in the battle.

The battle was fought on 19 January 1643 and was a victory for the Royalist Army commanded by Sir Ralph Hopton. Earlier they had been forced to retreat in the face of a superior Parliamentarian army due to lack of powder and arms. However, when three Parliamentarian warships sheltered at Falmouth harbour to escape a storm on 17 January 1643, they were captured by the Royalists who thus replenished their stocks. Hopton then decided to lead an attack against Scotsman Lord Ruthin and his Parliamentarian troops.

The Royalists discovered the Parliamentarians at Braddock Down. Hopton had more infantry than Ruthin, however, the Parliamentarians had more cavalry. Once Hopton decided to attack, after revealing to the Parliamentarians that he had two light canons, Sir Bevil Grenville and his Cornish foot army charged the Parliamentarians with such force that it caused them to flee. They had only fired a single volley which managed to kill two Royalists who were the only casualties on their side. The escaping Parliamentarians reached Liskeard where the men of the town turned on them. The pursuing Royalists succeeded in capturing approximately 1,500 men together with arms and powder and five invaluable guns.

Meanwhile, Saltash had also suffered from heavy bombardment from the river. The fighting resulted in much bloodshed in the town and damage to many buildings. Plymouth was a Roundhead town and most of the damage was done to Saltash as Cromwell's army tried to get a foothold in Cornwall. This is the reason why many of the Tudor and Jacobean properties that once existed in Saltash are no longer there.

At the end of the Civil War, Saltash declined as Plymouth and Devonport gained importance. The remains of a Royalist Civil War battery can still be found beside the lane leading down to Wearde Quay.

The Regatta was first recorded in 1835, although there had probably been regattas taking place before that year. Families living on Waterside have rowed their boats well before the Normans built Trematon Castle and races probably took place before the first recorded event. One of the most successful and well-known rowers in the Regatta was Ann Glanville. Between 1830 and 1850, she and her all-women crew competed in regattas all over Britain and were rarely beaten.

Born in 1796 in Saltash, she was the daughter of a waterman. She married young and had fourteen children. One of her characteristics was that she stood over 6ft tall. Together with her husband, she ran the ferry between Saltash and St Budeaux. When her husband fell ill and could no longer work, Ann carried on running the ferry so that she could support her family. She also delivered goods by water and would row between Sutton Pool and Budshead Mill, a distance of about 10 miles.

In her spare time, she put together a crew of female rowers from Saltash and they entered the 1833 Plymouth Regatta and took second place. Over the next fifteen years, the crew were the main contenders in many races around Britain. They had financial backers, including a Mr Waterman and Captain Russell who was in charge of the steamer, *Brunswick*.

They were hardly ever beaten even when they were up against male competitors. When they rowed in a race in Le Havre in 1842, the male competing team withdrew saying that it would be unchivalrous for them to compete against an all-female team. However, in truth, the probable reason for their withdrawal was that they knew they would be beaten. Ann Glanville died in 1878, aged 82, and is buried at St Stephen's.

The Regatta continued into the early 1900s and 1909 was a highlight when HRH The Prince of Wales presented a cup to the winners. During the First World War, the event stopped but was resumed as soon as the war ended and it continued until the start of the Second World War. After the war the Regatta continued and still runs today, as popular as it ever was.

In the late 1800s, the town was chosen as the crossing place for Brunel's Royal Albert Bridge and many of the people of Saltash began to commute regularly to Plymouth to work, particularly in the thriving dockyard. The town grew as the population rose sharply. When it was decided to also build the Tamar Road Bridge, 100 years later, Saltash became the main gateway to Cornwall and the population again grew as a result.

Many of the older buildings remain in Saltash although none so old as Mary Newman's Cottage in Culver Road. Tudor buildings were either destroyed during the Civil War, during the Second World War or by modern redevelopment. Much has disappeared over the years. Gone are the dwellings at Waterside and the thriving community in the area once affectionately called Picklecockle Alley. Also lost are the buildings removed during the construction of the Tamar Road Bridge and the Saltash Tunnel. Many industries have also disappeared in the last hundred years or so including quarrying, ship building and fishing. The limekilns have disappeared, as have the gasworks. Gone too are the tea gardens, the coal merchants, the brass and iron foundries and of course, the ferry.

The Royal Naval Torpedo School, HMS *Defiance*, was established in 1884. The ninth vessel to be called HMS *Defiance* was launched in 1861 but it was considered obsolete, because of the new iron clad ships, so it was towed to Plymouth to become part of the reserve fleet. Stripped of machinery, she was moored in the Hamoaze, off Wearde Quay where she became the new Torpedo School training ship.

Lower Fore Street, Saltash in Victorian times. Parts of Fore Street have changed considerably over the years although this area is still easy to recognise.

Perseus was moored near to *Cambridge* and was joined to *Defiance* by a walkway. The upper deck of *Defiance* included a lecture room, officers' rooms and a gymnasium. The lower deck housed the ship's company. A recreation room included magazines, newspapers and even a billiard table.

When Isambard Kingdom Brunel built the Royal Albert Bridge in 1859, he changed the face of Cornwall forever. The rail link meant that many residents of Saltash began to commute to Plymouth on a regular basis.

The town grew in size as the population rose because of the easy rail access. Perhaps, nowadays, the bridge is seen as a great boon for Saltash but at the time, many residents weren't happy about the new addition. Some called it 'an iron monstrosity' which they felt ruined the look of the once tranquil river. Others disliked the extra visitors to their small town. There was now easy access to Saltash whereas before people would have had to travel across the small ferry. Now, visitors could travel down in great numbers from all over the country and not just to Saltash, but also to anywhere in Cornwall and this had a great affect on the area.

The Saltash Station opened on 4 May 1859 and was part of the broad gauge Cornwall Railway. The Great Western Railway took over the Cornwall Railway on 1 July 1889. In July 1904, with competition from trams, small stations were opened to run local services between Saltash, Plymouth and Plympton. The station became the busiest in Cornwall and an amazing 56,000 people were using it a month. On average 1,800 used it daily, most of these being dockyard workers. The busy station was also responsible for the despatch of market produce from the Tamar Valley. With almost thirty trains a day serving Saltash and with so many tickets being issued, the station became the first to have a mini-printer machine installed in 1955. As cars became more popular and with the opening of the Tamar Road Bridge in 1961, services were vastly reduced.

When the Second World War broke out in 1939, thousands of children were evacuated to safe areas around the country, one of which was Saltash. However, Saltash wasn't as safe as many had thought and when Plymouth suffered its first attack in 1940, Saltash residents found themselves hastily hurrying to their own private air-raid shelters or to the public shelters located at Brunel Green, Alexandra Square, Fore Street and Victoria Gardens. Barrage balloons flew over Wearde, the Warfelton Cricket Pitch, Shillingham and Pill and an anti-aircraft battery was set up at Carkeel.

By 1941 stray bombs started to land in the countryside around Saltash from German planes returning from bombing raids on Plymouth. Saltash suffered its first casualties when one of their fire engines rushed to give aid after a bombing attack on Plymouth. Unfortunately, the crew were caught up in a bombing raid at King Street in Stonehouse. All six firemen were killed instantaneously. The Royal Albert Bridge was a definite target, which would have severely disrupted rail traffic had it been hit. Luckily, the bridge remained undamaged though an armaments barge was hit which caused casualties and severe damage to the surrounding area.

During April 1941 several incendiary and high explosive bombs fell on Saltash killing seven residents and destroying over twenty buildings. All the churches in the area suffered some sort of damage as well as the North Road School. The Imperial Picture House was completely destroyed as was the Wesley Church, Fore Street's last surviving Tudor building and a GWR goods station. Nearby streets that were hit included Port View, Glebe Avenue and Belle Vue Road.

With the heavy bombing of Plymouth, residents headed out of the city and travelled across to Saltash by train or by the ferry to escape the attacks. There were no rest centres prepared in Saltash and many people went out into the country for safety. However, townsfolk, especially residents of St Stephen's Road, which was the main route away from the town, offered Plymothians their sitting rooms as a place to sleep. From Saltash, the terrible attack on Plymouth could be seen clearly. By 28 April 1941, Saltash had heard the sound of the air raid alarm 100 times since the beginning of the year.

Sand Quay was used as a wartime base for American landing craft which were then used during the landings on D-Day.

Today, Saltash is still a popular town with a busy shopping area around Fore Street and has many attractions including parks and country walks such as those found at the nearby Churchtown Farm, Forder and Antony Passage.

Callington lies 7 miles north of Saltash and has a population of about 5,800. It has been suggested that the town is one of the possible locations of the ancient site of Celliwig, once the court of King Arthur. The name Celliwig translates to Forest Grove. Close by are the ancient monuments of Castlewitch Henge and Cadsonbury Iron Age hillfort. Dupath Well is also located nearby and was built on the site of an ancient spring in 1510.

The town was mentioned in the Domesday Book of 1086 when it was recorded that the manor had '4 hides of land and land for 30 ploughs'. The income from the manor was £6.

The view today looking towards the waterfront at Saltash. Flint arrowheads and skin scrapers dating back from 4,000 to 1,500BC have been found in the fields around Saltash. There was also possibly a Roman settlement on the Saltash side of the ferry crossing.

Tavistock Road, Callington. The silver mine at Callington became one of the most important mines in Great Britain during the nineteenth century.

After silver deposits were found in the nineteenth century, Callington became one of the most important mines in Great Britain. Remains of past mining lie in Silver Valley, and, although no active silver mines are in use today, granite continues to be mined at Hingston Down.

St Mary's Church in Callington was consecrated in 1438 and was formerly a chapel of ease to South Hill. Originally, it contained two aisles and a buttressed tower with a second north aisle being added in 1882. The tomb and effigy of Robert Willoughby, 1st Baron Willoughby de Broke, who died in 1502, can be found within its walls.

Launceston is recorded in the Domesday Book which mentions that it was held by the Count of Mortain who had a castle there. The name 'Launceston' means the 'church enclosure of St Stephen'. The former monastery of St Stephen's is situated to the north-west of the town. The original name of the castle and town was Dunheved.

Stonegate Arch in Launceston in the 1950s. The motte-and-bailey castle at Launceston was built in 1070 during Norman times by Robert, the Count of Mortain.

During the time of Æthelred the Unready the earliest known Cornish mint operated at Launceston. Only one coin is known to exist from that time. The mint was moved to Dunheved in the reign of William the Conqueror and continued until the reign of Henry II. During the reign of Henry III, a further mint was established in the town.

The castle in Launceston is a motte-and-bailey castle which was built during Norman times by Robert, the Count of Mortain, in 1070. Robert was the half-brother of William the Conqueror.

The town was the head of the feudal barony of Launceston and of the Earldom of Cornwall. However, during the thirteenth century it was replaced by Lostwithiel. Launceston became the county town of Cornwall until 1835, when it was replaced by Bodmin.

Cuthbert Mayne, a Roman Catholic martyr, was executed at Launceston.

During the English Civil War Launceston sided with Charles I and the Royalist cause. In 1643, Parliamentarian troops commanded by Major General James Chudleigh attempted to capture the town from the Royalists. Meanwhile, the Royalist commander, Ralph Hopton, 1st Baron Hopton, positioned his army on the summit of Beacon Hill, overlooking the town. The Parliamentarians managed to capture the foot of the hill, but were unable to defeat the Royalist army at the top. Hopton led an attack down the hill towards the Parliamentarians. Chudleigh received reinforcements but after the ensuing fight, the Parliamentarians were forced to retreat.

Sir Richard Grenville, refused to serve under Lord Hopton and was later sent to Launceston Prison for insubordination before being imprisoned on St Michael's Mount.

Liskeard is an ancient stannary and market town situated approximately 20 miles west of Plymouth, a stannary being a place where tin was mined.

After the Norman Conquest, a castle was built at Liskeard but it fell into disuse during the Middle Ages. It later became a house

Stuart House and Library, Liskeard. The town was once the centre of the tin mining industry and brought much prosperity to the area.

for the Earl of Cornwall but had fallen into disrepair by the time Sir Richard Carew visited it in 1602.

In 1240, a market charter was granted by Richard, Earl of Cornwall and brother of Henry III. Thereafter it became an important centre for agriculture.

Wilkie Collins, the novelist and playwright visited the town in the 1850s and described it as 'that abomination of desolation, a large agricultural country town'.

The boom in tin mining brought prosperity to the town and it became the centre for the industry as well as a location for a stannary and coinage.

Today, Liskeard is popular with shoppers and still has a regular livestock market held on every other Tuesday. A pantomime is put on in the last week of January and there is also a carnival held every June.

Looe, 20 miles west of Plymouth is a popular tourist coastal resort which also draws its living from the fishing trade. Archaeological evidence suggests that the area around Looe has been inhabited since 1,000BC. On a hill above East Looe is a stone circle, located at Bin Down. The name originates from 'Bin Dun' which, in Cornish means hill fort.

The bridge and harbour at Looe in the 1960s. The current bridge was built in Victorian times and opened in 1853.

In the time of the Domesday Book of 1086 much of the area fell within the manor of Pendrym which, at the time, was held by William the Conqueror. The land was later devolved to the Bodgrugan (Bodrigan) family. Across the river, the land belonged to the manors of Portalla and Portbyhan.

Shutta, close to East Looe, was inhabited in the twelfth century. Between 1154 and 1189, a charter was granted by Henry II which favoured Sir Henry Bodrugan as Mayor of East Looe. Shortly after, West Looe was given free borough status. From 1230, East Looe received the rights to hold a regular weekly market and a Michaelmas fair.

Nearby Looe Island was occupied by Benedictine monks some time before 1144 and they built a chapel there as well as a basic lighthouse. Another chapel was built just outside West Looe. Only ruins remain of both buildings. A chapel of ease existed in Looe as well as a parish church at St Martin at East Looe. In 1259, Walter Bronescombe, the Bishop of Exeter, dedicated the Church of St Mary in East Looe. In 1347, Looe provided twenty ships which were used at the Siege of Calais.

In medieval times, near the centre of the bridge, the Chapel of St Anne stood and was dedicated in 1436. Originally, a wooden bridge crossed the Looe River and was in place by 1411. However, it burned down and was replaced by a stone bridge which was finished in 1436, complete with chapel. The current bridge was built in Victorian times and opened in 1853. Looe had become a major port by this time and exported tin, arsenic and granite. The fishing and boatbuilding industry also thrived.

The town prospered during the Middle Ages and Tudor period and the port was easily accessible from the main Penzance to London road. The town's economy was increased by the textile trade as well as the trade from fishing, including especially pilchards and crabs. Goods were transported back and forth to the newly-thriving Newfoundland.

Looe's prosperity declined at the beginning of the 1800s. The Napoleonic Wars had drained the resources of much of the country. During 1803, Looe engaged a company of volunteers to man guns to defend the area against a French attack.

In 1808, a blockade stopped the Looe fleet from harvesting its pilchard fishing stocks which put a substantial strain on the community. The town was badly damaged by storms in 1817 which resulted in much flooding.

When the Liskeard and Looe Union Canal opened in 1828, it linked the two communities. Copper mining became prosperous in the area from 1837 and revived Looe's fortunes. Between 1848 and 1884, the mine at Herodsfoot produced 13,470 tons together with 17 tons of silver between 1853 and 1884.

Lime was transported on the canal which was brought from Wales to aid Cornish farming. Later, the canal was used to carry copper and granite between Liskeard and Looe. By 1856 a larger quay had been built at East Looe to cope with the increased shipping trade. In 1860, a railway was built linking Looe to Moorswater and was located along the towpath of the canal which was used less and less until it ceased being used in 1910.

The Lifeboat station at East Looe beach was originally established in 1866. The guildhall in Looe was built twelve years later in 1878.

In 1879, when the mining boom came to an end, the railway was linked properly to Liskeard and began carrying passengers. Looe became popular with tourists during Victorian times with the railway making it more accessible and Looe's prosperity grew with the new trade from holidaymakers.

Four miles west of Looe is the tiny fishing village of **Polperro** which is very popular with holidaymakers and includes many original fishermen's houses dating back hundreds of years. From medieval times, Polperro has fallen under the jurisdiction of two ancient and separate manors – Lansallos, west of the River Pol, and Killigarth which lies to the east as part of the parish of Talland.

Polperro was noted as a fishing settlement as early as the thirteenth century and was first recorded in a Royal document of 1303.

In 1708, the East Indiaman *Albemarle*, carrying a valuable cargo of diamonds, coffee, pepper, silk and indigo, was forced ashore by strong winds. Today the location of the wreck still lies undiscovered.

The harbour was built some time before 1774 when it was noted that it was damaged by a violent storm. The repairs were paid for by Thomas Long, of Penheale and lord of the manors of Raphael and Lansallos. An older harbour had stood on the site previously. Another storm in 1817 destroyed parts of the harbour but they were rebuilt. Thirty larger vessels, two seiners and various smaller boats were destroyed in the storm as well as many other parts of the village, including the Green and Peak Rock which were overwhelmed by the sea. Several houses were also swept away. At the time, the cost of the damage was estimated at £2,000. Fortunately, no lives were lost. The powerful storm also caused damage to property from Plymouth to Land's End.

A meeting of local fishermen at Polperro. The village was a noted fishing settlement as far back as the thirteenth century and was first recorded in a royal document in 1303.

In 1824 Polperro was hit by its worst storm and three houses were completely destroyed along with the whole of one pier and half of the other along with fifty boats in the harbour. The new pier was designed to give better protection to the village.

Smuggling prospered in Polperro from as early as the twelfth century. It peaked in the late eighteenth century when Britain was at war with America and France. This led to high taxation of many imported goods and made it profitable for local fishermen to increase their income by bringing in goods such as spirits and tobacco from Guernsey and other areas. Zephaniah Job (1749–1822) was a local merchant known as the 'Smugglers' Banker'. He operated in the area in the late eighteenth century and controlled much of the trade.

During the next century, a more efficiently organised Coast Guard service was set up and stiffer penalties were introduced which ultimately led to the decline of smuggling.

In 1807 Robert Jeffery, who resided at Polperro, was found guilty of stealing his midshipman's beer while aboard HMS *Recruit* in the charge of Commander Warwick Lake. Lake abandoned Jeffrey on the island of Sombrero. Jeffery had been born in Falmouth but moved to Polperro before he joined the merchant navy. He was later press-ganged into the Royal Navy. Lake's commanding officer, Sir Alexander Cochrane, heard about Jeffrey's misadventure several months later and immediately ordered Lake to rescue him. When HMS *Recruit* arrived back at Sombrero, Jeffery was nowhere to be found. When the story got out, Lake was court martialed and dismissed from the Royal Navy.

Eventually, it was discovered that Jeffery had been rescued by an American ship and later found work as a blacksmith in Massachusetts. He was eventually repatriated to Britain where he was awarded compensation for his ordeal.

Fowey is a small town located at the mouth of the River Fowey. It lies at the entrance of a large flooded valley which was created after the last ice age when the sea level rose dramatically.

Local legend says that Jesus Christ once visited Fowey as a child, accompanied by Joseph of Arimathea, who was a merchant with an interest in the town's tin mines. A cross marks their landing point below the cliffs to the south-west of St Saviour's Point. Many early charts show the cross which was maintained by monks from Tywardreath. Locally, the cross is known as Punches Cross which is said to derive from the name, Pontius Pilate.

At the end of the eleventh century the Domesday Book records manors at Penventinue and Trenant. At Tywardreath, a priory was established. A charter was granted to the people of Fowey by the prior in 1300. Fowey in medieval times ran from the northern gate near Boddinick Passage towards the southern gate which lay where Lostwithiel Street now stands. The town extended up the hillside and was bounded by the river. Merchants' houses backed onto the waterfront.

Trade developed with Europe using the natural harbour. Local ship owners leased their vessels to the king during various wars. At the

Tall ships at Fowey. Local legend states that Jesus Christ once visited Fowey as a child, accompanied by Joseph of Arimathea, who was a merchant with an interest in the town's tin mines.

same time, the town became well-known for piracy and a local group of privateers known as the 'Fowey Gallants' were granted a licence to seize French vessels and their cargo during the Hundred Years' War.

The harbour was defended by 160 archers during the 1300s and later, two blockhouses were built on both sides of the entrance to the harbour. In 1457 the town was attacked by French forces. At the time, Place House was defended against the invading army but was strengthened soon after in anticipation of a further attack.

In 1540, a castle was built on St Catherine's Point. The Dutch attacked in 1667 but were unable to get past the coastal defences and were successfully repelled.

During the English Civil War, Fowey sided with the Royalists. However, in 1644, a Parliamentarian army, led by the Earl of Essex, marched to Lostwithiel and were positioned around Fowey. During August the Royalist forces surrounded Essex's army. Charles I viewed Fowey from Hall Walk above Polruan, where he was nearly killed by a stray musket shot. The Parliamentary cavalry managed to force their way through the Royalist lines on 31 August and headed back towards Saltash. The foot soldiers were left behind, their only escape being by sea. The Earl of Essex and some officers managed to get away, but most of the force surrendered at Golant. They were marched to Poole but many died before they reached there.

Much trade left the harbour at Fowey and was taken over by larger towns such as Plymouth. Fishing became a far more important trade in the area and local merchants were appointed as privateers and carried out smuggling on the side.

Important industries in the area included the mining of tin, copper and iron and the quarrying of china clay. Rival harbours were improved due to the increased trade, with West Polmear beach becoming Charlestown Harbour in 1800. The same thing took place at Pentewan in 1826.

Copper was shipped from Caffa Mill Pill, near Fowey by Joseph Austen before work started on the new Par harbour in 1829. It was another forty years before the harbour at Fowey was developed but it gained an advantage over other harbours with its natural deep water anchorage and its connection to the railway. To improve navigation, a beacon was erected at Gribben Head by Trinity House to guide vessels into Fowey harbour and around the bay at Par.

In 1869 an Act of Parliament allowed the Fowey Harbour Commissioners to enlarge and improve the harbour. The broad gauge Lostwithiel and Fowey Railway was opened on 1 June of that year leading to large jetties at Carne Point. The railway initially carried just goods, but in 1876 a passenger railway was opened on the Cornwall Minerals Railway on reclaimed land at Caffa Mill Pill. Towards the end of 1879, the Lostwithiel line was closed but reopened by the Cornwall Minerals Railway in 1895. In 1934 the passenger lines to Par were discontinued and in 1965, the passenger line ceased to Lostwithiel. The Par line later became a roadway used specifically by lorries carrying china clay.

Famous residents included Daphne du Maurier (1907–1989) the author and playwright famous for her stories including *Rebecca* and *Jamaica Inn*; Mabel Lucie Attwell (1879–1964), illustrator; Kenneth Grahame (1859–1932), author, best known for *The Wind in the Willows*, who lived in Fowey for part of the year; and Mary Bryant who was born in Fowey in 1765 before later being transported as a convict to the penal colony in New South Wales, Australia. She became one of the first people to escape.

CHAPTER 2

The Rame Peninsula

The Rame Peninsula is a beautiful part of Cornwall generally missed by tourists who travel further down into the heart of the county. For this reason, the area is known as the Forgotten Corner. The area can be reached by ferry to Torpoint, by foot ferry to Cremyll and by road via the Tamar Bridge.

Torpoint is a small town which was designed in 1774 for Reginald Pole Carew, a British politician who lived at Antony House. It is linked to Plymouth by the Torpoint ferry.

In 1796 the crew of the government ship, the *Viper*, had a fierce gun battle with a group of smugglers in Torpoint. One person was killed and five were seriously injured.

A Victorian view of the Torpoint ferry. The town was designed in 1774 for Reginald Pole Carew, a British politician who lived at Antony House.

The town grew as workers from the dockyard at nearby Devonport settled there and when the Royal Naval training facility, HMS *Raleigh*, was established. Today, it is more built up with a popular shopping area as well as three schools and Non-League football club, Torpoint Athletic FC, who play at The Mill.

Wilcove is a small village situated a mile north of Torpoint in the civil parish of Antony. The village had strong connections to the agricultural trade and included two farms, Whitehall Farm and Home Farm. These employed many people living in the village. After the war, the Bullock Diamond Factory, which later became Select Gauges, was situated in the village. There are links to the Royal Navy with HMS *Defiance*, a naval base, being situated in the village until the 1950s. HMS *Valiant* was moored off the village between the First and Second World Wars. Thanckes oil depot is housed in the south-east part of the village and belongs to the Ministry of Defence.

The small village of **Antony** lies 3 miles west of Torpoint. In 1086 the Domesday Book records that the manor of Antony belonged to Ermenhald of Tavistock Abbey. A medieval parish church, parts of which date from the thirteenth, fourteenth and fifteenth centuries, lies in the village and is dedicated to St James. Included within the church are memorials to members of the Carew family. There is also a large monumental brass dedicated to Margery Arundell in 1420.

Richard Carew (1555–1620), the author of the book, *A Survey of Cornwall*, once lived in the village.

Nearby **Antony House** was built in the early 1700s and today belongs to the National Trust. Sir William Carew had the house built between 1718 and 1724. The estate has been owned by the Carew family since the mid-1500s and remains their main residence. The house and gardens were given to the National Trust in 1961 with the stipulation that the family would continue to live there. Tremayne Carew Pole currently lives there with his family.

An early photo showing the village of Antony. Richard Carew (1555–1620), the author of the book, A Survey of Cornwall, *once lived in the village.*

Antony House in the 1950s. Sir William Carew had the house built between 1718 and 1724.

In 2008, Disney filmed *Alice in Wonderland* on the estate. The movie was directed by Tim Burton and starred Johnny Depp, as well as many local extras.

Sheviock lies in the St Germans Registration district and the parish is bordered by St Germans creek to the north. The parish church of St Mary's dates from the thirteenth century, although further building work took place in the next two centuries. The are two tombs dating back to the fourteenth century which are believed to have belonged to the Courtenay family. The stained-glass panels were designed by George Edmund Street who was responsible for restoring the church in 1850.

At the crossroads between Sheviock Churchtown and Crafthole, there is a Cornish cross, known locally as Stump Cross.

The village of **St John** is 1½ miles south-east of Torpoint. The site of an Iron Age castle lies on high ground called Vanderbands, several hundred metres north of the village. A church existed in the area in 1080 although records were destroyed when the Mount Edgcumbe Estate was bombed in the Second World War. The current church was built in 1150 and was originally dedicated to St John the Evangelist, however, in 1490 it was re-dedicated to John the Baptist. Much of the church was built in the fifteenth century and only the western tower survives from the Norman period.

During the 1850s, the navy sited its gunnery school on the Hamoaze. Known as HMS *Cambridge*, it consisted of two hulks which fired cannonballs towards a target at St John's Lake. Today, the lake is littered with these cannonballs which can be seen at low tide. Many collectors have recovered them although it can be a messy and dangerous task.

Southdown lies on the banks of the Hamoaze to the east of Millbrook. Its quay was originally built as a naval victualling yard before becoming a brickworks. Today, it's the home to Southdown Marina.

Southdown and the Hamoaze. The quay at Southdown was originally built as a naval victualling yard before becoming a brickworks.

Insworke, which was previously also known as Inceworth, is a small hamlet which lies in the parish of Millbrook. Before 1869 it lay in the parish of Maker. From 1319, a fair and annual market were held there.

The village of **Milbrook** is within the boundaries of the Rame Peninsula and during the 1800s, and before, was a thriving fishing village. It was once a market town where fairs were held, each year on 1 May and 29 September. Sir John Cornwall was given the title of Lord of Millbrook by Henry VIII but records show that the village existed before then and mention is made of it in 1442 (during the reign of Henry VI). During the reign of Elizabeth I, the village had forty fishing boats and men sailed from the village to fight in various wars during this period.

Involvement with the brick making and terra cotta manufacturing industries, as well as the flourishing smelting works in the village, saw an increase in workers moving to the area. The smelting of copper ceased about 1904 but brick production continued between 1885 and 1956, when Southdown Brick Company closed down.

An early scene showing Millbrook. Involvement with the brickmaking and terra cotta manufacturing industries as well as the flourishing smelting works in the village saw an increase in workers moving to the area.

The windmill at Empacombe. John Rudyerd lived at Empacombe in 1706 together with his Eddystone Lighthouse workshop. Rudyerd's lighthouse was built of wood and was completed in 1709.

Anderton forms part of Millbrook and is situated on the tidal part of Millbrook Lake on the Tamar estuary. Following the road around and the country path leads to **Empacombe**, home of the Earl of Mount Edgcumbe. John Rudyerd, a Cornish-born London-based silk merchant, lived at Empacombe in 1706 together with his Eddystone Lighthouse workshop. Rudyerd's lighthouse was built of wood and was completed in 1709. It was the second Eddystone lighthouse to be built. The first, built by Winstanley, was swept away in a storm in 1703 and Rudyerd's lighthouse was destroyed by fire in 1755. Two shipwrights called Smith and Northcutt were employed to help him design the building.

The 1881 Census shows that a George Brighton lived at Empacombe with his daughters, Clara and Emily. He was 60 years old at the time and was employed as head gardener at Mount Edgcumbe. Other people living at Empacombe included George Adams, aged 27, who lived with his wife, Hannah, and daughter, Jessie. He was also employed as a gardener on the Mount Edgcumbe Estate. Other residents included Charles Penprase, a 30-year-old agricultural labourer, his wife Mary, aged 31, and his mother, Ann, aged 68, and Samuel Harvey, aged 70, a land agent, and his family.

There is an Empacombe Battery which was constructed in 1803 and is built of stone. It is also known as the Maker Redoubt No.6. An old windmill, dating from the 1700s, stands on the hill nearby.

Following the footpath from Empacombe leads down to **Cremyll**. The Cremyll Ferry originated during Saxon times. It first appears in documentation in 1204, in the papers of Reginald de Valletort, and was one of the major crossing routes between Devon and Cornwall. The rights to the ferry were, at the time, granted to Ralph Edgcumbe and the family continued to lease them out until 1943 when the Millbrook Steamboat and Trading Company took over. It was then bought by the company from the Edgcumbe family in 1945.

The ferry originally left from a slipway at Devil's Point and landed on the Cremyll shore near to where the Passage House and Gardens

once stood, on the spot where the Orangery at Mount Edgcumbe is now. The Passage House, the gardens and Schillhall Cottage were leased with the ferry rights until the Italian Garden was laid out in the 1700s. The landing place was then moved northwards.

The ferry journey could be a dangerous and trying one especially with the strong currents. Celia Fiennes, who lived at the same time as Daniel Defoe, wrote of her tour in 1698 between Plymouth and Penzance. She mentions the journey to Cremyll, which at the time was called 'Crilby':

From Plymouth I went one mile to Crilby Ferry which is a very hazardous crossing passage by reason of three tides meeting. Had I known the danger before, I would not have been very willing to have gone on it, not but this is the constant way most people go and saves several miles riding. I was at least an hour going over and it was about a mile, but indeed in some places, notwithstanding there were five men rowing and I set

my own men to row also, I do believe that we made almost not
a step of the way for a quarter of an hour, but blessed by God
I came safely over; but those ferry boats are so wet and the sea
is always so cold to be upon that I never fail to catch cold in
a ferry boat as I did this day, having two more ferries to cross,
tho' none so bad or half so long as this. Thence to Millbrook,
2 miles, and went all along by the water and had the full view
of the dockyards.

The Rame Register of 1701 reports that six women and a man were
drowned at Crimble on 26 July.The fares for the ferry in 1810 were
five shillings for a coach with four horses and a guinea for a hearse
with a coffin.

Louis Duprez wrote, in his *Visitors' Guide to Mount Edgcumbe*,
published in 1871, that, *'the beach is crowded with hundreds of visitors*
and boatmen are vociferating loudly in their zealous endeavour
to embark as many fares as possible. There are gingerbread and
sweetmeats stalls and trade is brisk at the Mount Edgcumbe Arms,
an old fashioned well-regulated house.'

In 1885, steam boats were introduced. These towed a horse boat
which, on many occasions, broke loose and had to be recovered down
river.

There has been a shipyard to the right of the Mount Edgcumbe
Arms for hundreds of years. It was taken over by Mashfords
in 1930 and during the Second World War, the company built
assault landing craft and anti-submarine motor launches for the
Admiralty. Mashfords have also had many famous customers
including Sir Francis Chichester, Sir Alec Rose and Ann Davison
who, at the age of 39, was the first woman to single-handedly sail
the Atlantic. She left Plymouth on 18 May 1952 in the boat, *The*
Felicity Ann, which was purpose-built by Mashford Brothers Ltd.
Work commenced on the boat in 1939 but was delayed by the Second
World War and it wasn't launched until 1949.

Stonehouse was once known as East Stonehouse to distinguish it from the hamlet of West Stonehouse which stood on the opposite side of the river, near to Cremyll, which was said to have been burnt down by the French in the 1350s. West Stonehouse was originally owned by the ancient family, the Valletorts, and was in turn passed by marriage to the Durnford family before finally being passed to the Edgcumbe family as the dowry of Joan Durnford when she married Sir Piers Edgcumbe in 1493.

Carew wrote in his *Survey of Cornwall* in 1602:

Certaine old ruines yet remaining confirm the neighbours' report that near the water's side, there stood once a towne called West Stonehouse until the French by fire and sword overthrew it.

This passage refers to the Breton raids of the late 1300s and early 1400s. However, in *The Directory of Plymouth*, Stonehouse and Devonport by Robert Brindley, published in 1830, he states:

About 1730, Barnpool was removed for the annoyance which it caused to the lordly domain of Mount Edgcumbe, and at the same time, West Stonehouse which had a chapel and was inhabited by fishermen was razed by the owners of the lovely domain of Mount Edgcumbe and not destroyed by the French as generally supposed.

The accounts contradict each other but it is probable that West Stonehouse was destroyed by the French and the place referred to in Brindley's Directory refers to the remains of the hamlet. These remains would have been cleared away when the formal gardens were laid out in the 1700s. The small chapel that was at Barn Pool was said to have been removed and placed in the Picklecombe Valley and formed part of Picklecombe Seat.

West Stonehouse, or its remains, were still in existence in 1515 when King Henry VIII granted Sir Piers Edgcumbe a royal licence to keep deer at 'Westonehouse and Cremele'.

Joshua Reynolds was said to have completed his first portrait at the age of 12 in a boat house at Cremyll in 1735. The story was told in *An Anecdote Biography* by John Timbs in 1860. It makes interesting reading, not just for the connection between Reynolds and Cremyll but it also shows the friendship that existed between Reynolds and Richard Edgcumbe:

Reynolds' first portrait was painted when he could not have been more than twelve years old. It was the portrait of the Reverend Thomas Smart, in whose family the tradition is that in 1735, a young Joshua coloured the likeness in a boat-house at Cremyll beach under Mount Edgcumbe, on canvas which was part of a boat-sail, and with the common paint used by shipwrights. Mr Smart was the tutor in the family of Richard Edgcumbe, Esq, who afterwards became the first Lord Edgcumbe, the 'Dick Edgcumbe' of Walpole's correspondence; and young Reynolds seems to have been passing the holidays at Mount Edgcumbe with one of his sons. The portrait is said to have been painted from a drawing taken in church, and on the artist's thumb-nail: Hogarth was wont to sketch in a similar manner. The picture was for many years at Mount Edgcumbe, but was afterwards sent to Plympton, and hung up in one of the rooms belonging to the Corporation, of which Mr Smart was a member. It was subsequently returned to Mount Edgcumbe, and given by the present Earl to Mr Boger, of Wolsdon, the descendant and representative of Mr Smart, by whom these circumstances were related to Mr Cotton. This portrait has been accurately engraved by S.W. Reynolds.

Mr Boger has also a small portrait or panel of the daughter of Mr Smart, which is supposed to have been painted by Reynolds. At the above time, Mr Edgcumbe was one of the patrons of the Borough of Plympton, which accounts for the acquaintance between the boys. Young Richard Edgcumbe had also a good deal of taste for drawing, and some of his paintings are still at Mount Edgcumbe. He became one of Walpole's constant Christmas and Easter guests at

Strawberry Hill; and Reynolds, who painted the tutor on sail-cloth, in 1735, in his boyhood, likewise painted young Edgcumbe for Walpole, when he had reached the zenith of his fame, in a charming picture with Selwyn and Gilly Williams. Walpole describes this picture as by far one of the best things Reynolds had executed: it is engraved in Cunningham's edition of Walpole's Letters; the original picture, a little larger than cabinet size, was bought by the Right Honorable Henry Labouchere, now Lord Taunton, at the Strawberry Hill sale, in 1842. There is also at Mount Edgcumbe a portrait of Richard Lord Edgcumbe, painted by Sir Joshua when he was an untaught boy at Plympton, and before he went to London.

Cremyll has had many different names over the years including Crimela (1201), Cremill (1512), Crilby (1698), Crimbel (1701) and later, Crimhill.

HMS *Impregnable* was moored off Cremyll until 1906. The wooden battleship was launched in 1860 and, apart from trials, it never went to sea. Over a period of 25 years, she sat in the Hamoaze before being used as a Naval training ship. Originally called *Howe*, she was renamed in 1885 and then became the *Bulwark*. In 1886, her name was changed again, this time to *Impregnable*. In 1906, she was joined by the *Inconstant* and *Black Prince* before being moved further up river.

The **Mount Edgcumbe Estate** became a very popular destination for visitors during Victorian and Edwardian times. Steamboat trips left the Hoe and Waterside at Saltash laden with passengers including Sunday School teachers complete with picnic hampers. Others would row across from Stonehouse Creek and spend long summer days exploring the park.

The estate, complete with ornate gardens, has been popular with visitors for many years. In 1493, Sir Piers Edgcumbe married Joan Durnford and her dowry included land on both sides of the Tamar. In 1515, King Henry VIII granted Piers permission to empark deer on

Mount Edgcumbe House in the 1800s. In 1493 Sir Piers Edgcumbe married Joan Durnford and her dowry included land on both sides of the Tamar. In 1515 King Henry VIII granted Piers permission to empark deer on the land now known as Mount Edgcumbe.

the land now known as Mount Edgcumbe and between 1547 and 1553, Sir Richard Edgcumbe of Cotehele added a new home to the deer park.

Adjacent to the house is the Earl's Garden which was laid out in the eighteenth century. Contained in the garden are many ancient and rare trees including a Mexican Pine, a Lucombe Oak and a 400-year-old Lime. At the far end of the garden is an ornamental shell seat.

The ornamental gardens near the Orangery were a wilderness garden during the seventeenth century. However, during the eighteenth century, the Italian, French and English gardens were laid out.

After his defeat, Napoleon requested that he be imprisoned at Mount Edgcumbe House, but this request was denied and he was exiled to the Island of St Helena instead.

The Orangery as it is today at Mount Edgecumbe. A busy café now occupies the building. The Orangery was built in 1760 to house orange trees from Constantinople. Unfortunately, when it was bombed in 1941, many of the trees, some of which were over 100 years old, were destroyed. It was restored in 1953.

The ruined remains of Mount Edgcumbe House after it was bombed in 1941. The outer walls remained but the interior had to be rebuilt and this work was completed in 1964.

During the Victorian and Edwardian times, Mount Edgcumbe proved to be very popular and was visited by royalty and the celebrities of the day. It was open to the public on every Monday. A Plymouth man, Sam Webber, used to lease out boats from Stonehouse Creek to people for 6d an hour. The boats were between 12ft and 18ft and young couples would row over to Mount Edgcumbe for the day.

Mount Edgcumbe House, was built of red stone, with a stucco finish, and survived for hundreds of years until it was the victim of a direct hit during a German bomb attack in 1941. The outer walls remained but the interior had to be rebuilt and this work was completed in 1964. Unfortunately, many family records, historical documents, pictures and artefacts were lost forever. Ironically, during the war years, Adolf Hitler had shown an interest in living at Mount Edgcumbe if Germany won the war.

During 1944, the US Army (110th Field Artillery of the 29th Infantry Division) occupied the area around Barn Pool before leaving for Normandy to take part in the D-Day landings. Evidence of their time there can still be seen today and remnants of the 'hards', that their vehicles drove over, can be found scattered on the beach. Soldiers' names can also be found carved into the trees nearby.

US soldiers leaving Barn Pool in preparation for D-Day in June 1944. Evidence of their time there can still be seen today and remnants of the 'hards',that their vehicles drove over, can be found scattered on the beach. Soldiers' names can also be found carved into the trees nearby.

After the war, Mount Edgcumbe Park was open to visitors on every Wednesday, on Bank Holidays and the last Saturday of the month.

When the estate was loaned paintings from the Lord Harmsworth collection, they showed the Italian Garden in all its original glory. The gardens are today laid out in the original style with elements such as the Agaves taken from one of the Nicholas Condy watercolours in the collection. Condy was a local artist who was born in Torpoint in 1793.

During 1971, the house and its grounds were sold to Cornwall County and Plymouth City Councils and the house was leased to the family.

Samuel Pepys, in 1683, described Mount Edgcumbe as *'a most beautiful place as ever was seen'*. However, Dr Johnson, referring to the view from Mount Edgecumbe, noted, *'though there is the grandeur of a fleet, there is also the impression of there being a dockyard, the circumstances of which are not agreeable.'*

It was thought that the town of Plymouth with its buildings and dockyard somehow spoiled the beautiful view.

Below the house is the beautifully tree-lined avenue leading up from Cremyll towards Mount Edgcumbe House. The trees consist of sycamore, sweet chestnut and horse chestnut. Many were lost in the great blizzard of 1891 which devastated areas of the estate including the beech plantation above Lady Emma's Cottage.

The Great Blizzard of March 1891 affected many parts of the country particularly the South West. Strong gales and heavy snowfall hit Cornwall, Devon, Dorset, Herefordshire and Kent. London was also hit by the gale force winds and snowfalls. Some drifts were 15ft high. The devastation left behind included uprooted trees and blown away fencing and roofs. The storms were so ferocious that much of Cornwall and Devon were cut off from the rest of Britain for four days between 9 and 13 March 1891. In this time, over 200 people were killed as well as 6,000 animals.

In the census of 1891, William Dent was listed as the head of 'Mount Edgcumbe Mansion'. William was the 4th Earl and was, at the time, shown as being widowed and living with his daughter, Lady Edith Hallaran, age 28. Also living at the house were John Duckett, aged 41, who was a valet and domestic servant, and David King, aged 28, who was a domestic servant and footman. The census names seventeen servants living at the house, although many more lived on various parts of the estate. Their jobs included steward room man, housekeeper, cook, ladies maid, house maid, kitchen maid, scullery maid and laundry maid.

Mount Edgcumbe has welcomed many famous visitors over the years including Napoleon III (1808–1873), Emperor of France and the nephew of Napoleon Bonaparte (1769–1821). After the end of the Franco-German War, Napoleon III stayed at Torquay with his son and visited the estate just three days before the Crown Prince of Prussia

(Emperor Frederick 1831–1888) arrived with his wife and sons, one of whom was to later become Wilhelm II (1859–1941), more notoriously known as Kaiser Bill who was vilified for causing the First World War. Once again, history is interwoven with connections between the English aristocracy and our German enemies. Of course, the bigger connection here was that Wilhelm II was the grandson of Queen Victoria.

As a guest of Richard Edgcumbe, Willem Van der Velde, the elder, (1611–1693) painted the *Royal Charles* while at Mount Edgcumbe. The *Royal Charles* was a ship captured by the Dutch in June 1667 during the second Anglo Dutch war of 1665 to 1667. The vessel features in many paintings of the time.

Dr Samuel Johnson (1709–1784) visited in 1762, and other guests who came to the estate included General Pasquale di Paoli, who has been described as the Che Guevara of the eighteenth century. Paoli was introduced to Dr Johnson by James Boswell (1740–1795) who was Johnson's biographer. David Garrick (1717–1779) was another famous visitor. Garrick was an actor and playwright who also managed theatre productions. He was a pupil and friend of Dr Johnson. Fanny Burney (1752–1840) also visited Mount Edgcumbe. She was a novelist and diarist and a member of the literary set associated with Dr Johnson. She also served as a lady-in-waiting to Queen Charlotte. Burney was admired by Jane Austen, as well as by Dr Johnson and David Garrick. Austen called her, *'England's first woman novelist'*. Burney's diaries were published posthumously in 1841 and gave an accurate description of life in the 1700s. The 2nd Baron, Richard (1716–1761) was a close friend of Horace Walpole as was his brother, George, the 1st Earl (1721–1795). George was also friends with Joshua Reynolds, David Garrick and John Opie and became part of the 'Strawberry Hill' set.

Strawberry Hill was the home of Horace Walpole (1717–1797) which he bought in 1748 and which was rebuilt gradually over the years. He was visited by many writers, actors and aristocrats.

Walpole was the 4th Earl of Orford and was a politician, a writer, an antiquarian and art historian. He was the son of Sir Robert Walpole and a cousin of Lord Nelson.

After the marriage of Richard, George's son, the 2nd Earl of Edgcumbe (1764–1839) to Sophia Hobart, Fanny Burney wrote, *'he is a most neat little beau and his face has the roses and lillies as finely blended as that of his pretty young wife.'*

Richard liked to take part in amateur dramatics and was a musician. He wrote the book, *Musical Reminiscences of the Earl of Mount Edgcumbe* which contained all the operas he'd heard from 1773 to 1823.

Unfortunately, when the house was bombed in 1941, many of the Edgcumbe family's possessions were destroyed. These included rare furniture and paintings. Three generations of the Edgcumbe family were painted by Joshua Reynolds and all but one of the paintings were destroyed.

Since apparently both Adolf Hitler and Herman Goering wanted Mount Edgcumbe House as their country retreat, neither would have been best pleased when it was destroyed.

In 1944, concrete roads were laid in preparation for the D-Day invasion.

After being bombed, the house was left as a shell until 1958. Adrian Gilbert Scott was commissioned to rebuild the house using concrete floors and a steel frame. After the Second World War, the house had the rendering removed from its walls leaving its present red sandstone appearance. The entrance at the north front still has its original sixteenth century doorway and is surrounded by late seventeenth century Doric pilasters and a pediment. The house is decorated in neo-Georgian style.

During the war, the railings from the house were taken away to help as part of the war effort. Railings were collected from all over the country to be melted down and used in munitions. Although this practice united communities in their search for scrap metal, none of it was ever used. Unfortunately, although the exercise was said to boost morale, many of the railings collected around the country were simply dumped.

On the Edgcumbe estate on a hill near to Cremyll lies the **Obelisk**. There is a story that the Obelisk was erected to celebrate the life of the Countess of Mount Edgcumbe's pet pig, Cupid. However, other sources say that the Obelisk was erected, in its current position, by Timothy Brett in 1770 in honour of his friend, George, the 3rd Baron of Edgcumbe. Brett was a former Commissioner of the Navy.

The Obelisk was originally sited where the Folly now stands. The 50ft monument had been used as a navigational point by various shipping in the Sound over the years. Cupid was said to have been buried in a gold casket beneath the obelisk when he died in 1768. In the book, *Animals' Graves and Memorials* by Jan Toms (Shire Publications 2006), it says that when the obelisk was moved to its present position, in 1770, nothing was found. However, the date of 1770 may be misleading as the obelisk appears in its present position on shipping maps as early as 1768.

As this was the year that Cupid died, it might be reasonable to assume that he is buried beneath the obelisk in its present position. It is known that Fern Dell on the estate once contained an urn that commemorated Cupid but this has long since disappeared. However, it is also recorded that Cupid was buried at Fern Dell and this was noted by George III and Queen Charlotte.

Cupid led a charmed life eating at the dinner table of the Edgcumbes and even accompanying the Countess, Emma Gilbert, on trips to London. The Edgcumbes' love of their pets can be seen at Fern Dell where many of them are buried. When a later Countess of Mount Edgcumbe, Caroline Georgia, died in 1909, she requested that a fountain be erected near the shore at Cremyll which bore the inscription, 'For the Doggies'.

In *A Complete Parochial History of the County*, published in 1870, it states, *'In the Cypress Grove is a monument to the memory of Timothy*

Brett Esq, one of the commissioners of the Navy, who, about the year 1770 erected the obelisk on the knoll near Cremyll as a memorial for his regard of his friend, George, the 3rd Baron of Edgcumbe.'

At the time, George was still alive and serving in the Royal Navy. During 1770, he was promoted to Vice Admiral and was appointed Vice Treasurer of Ireland.

Today, the obelisk is almost hidden away on a hill behind the Mount Edgcumbe Arms. There is no plaque on the monument to say who it is dedicated to and it has probably seen better days. It's hard to imagine now that it once stood where the folly stands.

To add to the confusion, the date, '1st July, 1867', has been carved into the base of the obelisk. Beside the date is the name, 'R.F. Crowther'. This mystery has, however, since been solved. Richard Crowther was in training during the 1860s on the boy's training ship, HMS *Impregnable* which was moored off Cremyll. One day, Richard wandered towards the obelisk from the training ship armed with a hammer and chisel and left the inscription and date. He was born in 1853 so would have been 14 years old in 1867 when he left his mark.

The Barrow can be found on the Edgcumbe estate and is a Bronze Age burial mound which dates from around 1,200BC. It was used as a prospect mound during the eighteenth century and was also used as a viewing point to enjoy the surrounding gardens, the park and the city of Plymouth. At one time it was used as a firing range and a military camp was situated close by.

There are many other Bronze Age settlements in the area. Bronze Age barrows can be found near to the cliff edge at Tregonhawke, Rame Head, and Wiggle Cliff near Whitsand Bay.

During the 1800s, it became a popular pastime for the wealthy and well educated to carry out the task of barrow digging. Although this pastime revealed many aspects of the land's history, untold damage was also done at the same time.

Children in Victorian times enjoying a dip in the sea. Rame Head can be seen in the background. Flint tools discovered in the Rame Head area suggest that people inhabited the region as long ago as the Mesolithic period.

Flint tools discovered in the **Rame Head** area suggest that people inhabited the region as long ago as the Mesolithic period. There is evidence of Bronze Age barrows all over Cornwall.

Barrows or tumuli, as they are sometimes known, consist of a mound of earth and stone placed over a grave. They can be found throughout the world. Tumulus is the Latin word for 'mound' or 'small hill'. There are many types of barrows and as well as the remains of the deceased, they can also contain pottery vessels and weapons and tools. During the Bronze Age, bodies were quite often cremated and placed in vessels which would then be set into the ground beneath the burial mound. Mounds were placed in areas of importance.

There seems to be no record of the barrow at Mount Edgcumbe being excavated though it is quite possible that, at one time, this has taken place. The Bronze-age horns which are kept in Mount Edgcumbe House are not from a local source but come from Ireland.

The Orangery was built in 1760 to house orange trees from Constantinople. Unfortunately, when it was bombed in 1941, many of the trees, some of which were over 100 years old, were destroyed. It was restored in 1953. In later years, the Orangery has been used as a cafe and restaurant.

The Italian Garden was laid out between 1750 and 1809. Its main features are the mermaid fountain, the statues of Apollo, Venus and Bacchus, the bust of Ludovico Ariosto, the neatly trimmed lawns and the fine array of orange trees. The mermaid fountain features in a Nicholas Condy painting of the Italian Garden dated 1816. The fountain was a gift which was given to Richard, the second Earl, by Lord Bessborough in 1809. Many of the statues displayed in the garden would have been gathered during Grand Tours of Europe and neighbouring countries. Richard, the 2nd Baron Edgcumbe (1716–1761) had his Grand Tour extended as a young man to curb his gambling habits. When he returned in 1744, after a seven year stay in Turkey, he brought with him orange trees and a collection of classical antiquities.

Richard had a relatively short life, dying in his middle forties, when he had only held the title for three years. He enjoyed drawing and poetry and was a close friend of Horace Walpole, the 4th Earl of Orford.

The statues of Venus, Apollo and Bacchus in the garden date from around 1785. Bacchus, or Dionysus, is the god of wine and ecstatic liberation. He was the youngest of the great Greek gods. The statues would have been collected during the time of George the

1st Earl of Mount Edgcumbe (1721–1795). He had a great interest in antiquities like his brother, Richard, the 2nd Baron. The statues would have been collected in the later part of his life when George was in his sixties. As a young man, George served in the Royal Navy rapidly rising in the ranks from midshipman to rear admiral in 1772.

Richard (1764–1839), the 2nd Earl and the son of George, spent time in Italy during his Grand Tour and he married Sophia Hobart in 1789. She died at the young age of 38 but they had five children who shared a love of gardens and trees. The Italian Garden, the French Garden and much of the plantations and drives were laid out during this time.

Interestingly, when the statue of Apollo, in the Italian Garden, was repaired in the 1990s, a Marigold glove was used as a mould to make a new hand.

At the end of the Italian Gardens is a bust of Ludovico Ariosto (1474–1535), a sixteenth-century Italian poet and the author of the Italian epic poem 'Orlando Furioso' (1532). The bust dates from 1785 and is one of the souvenirs from the family's Grand Tours of Europe which were used to enhance the courtyard. There are two tablets of white marble nearby; the first, underneath in Italian text, reads:

Vicino al lido donde a poco a poco
Si salendo in verso il colle ameno
Mirti e cedri e naranci, e lauri il loco
E mille altri souvi arbori han perio
Serpillo dall odorifero terreno
Tanta scarila, che'n mar sentive
La fa ogni vento, che, da terra sfare.

This translates as:

Near to the shore, from whence with soft ascent Rises the
pleasant hill, there is a place. With many an orange, cedar,

myrtle, bay, And every shrub of grateful scent adorn'd. The rose, the lily, crocus, serpolet. Such sweets diffuse the odoriferous ground, That from the land each gently breathing gale Wafts forth the balmy fragrance to the sea.

Towards the water, down from Mount Edgcumbe house, lies the Garden Battery which was originally a saluting point with twenty-one guns in place to greet visitors. It was restored in 1747 and was rebuilt between 1862 and 1863 as part of Plymouth's sea defences. During the Second World War, the battery was armed to defend the river during enemy attacks. This part of the battery is known as Queen Victoria's landing stage and it was commissioned by William Henry, the 4th Earl of Edgcumbe (1832–1917). The cast iron wrought work has the date, 1862 shown along with Victoria's monogram, 'V R'. In the background can be seen Devil's Point and the Royal William Yard.

The English Garden House on the estate was built in 1729 and was extended in 1820. The garden, laid out in 1770, contains irregular lawns and many rare trees including a magnolia, several Cork oaks, a Ginkgo, a Fox-glove tree, an Indian Bean tree, a Japanese Red Cedar, a Witch Hazel and a Mimosa. Although it is called the English Garden, it contains many shrubs that are not native to this country.

After the death of his dog, Richard, 1st Baron of Edgcumbe, had its skeleton mounted and displayed in a case within the English Garden House. He would often visit and talk to his deceased friend. When the dog's body was removed in the 1800s, and probably buried at Fern Dell, there were reports of ghostly scratching as if the dog was trying to get back into the Garden House.

The Garden House in 1729 would have formed part of the then wilderness garden. When the new garden was laid out in the 1770s, the house was used as a focal point. It has been used by the family for picnics and for listening to music. In 1820, it was extended to contain a room with a sunken bath and two new wings.

Close to the English Garden is the Rose Garden which dates from the late 1700s. Newer gardens include the American Garden, laid out in 1989, the New Zealand Garden, also laid out in 1989 and complete with geyser, and the Jubilee Garden which was completed in 2002.

The French Garden was laid out in 1803. It was surrounded by bay hedges with yew and oak trees. A statue of Mercury once stood at the far end of the garden and this was reflected in the convex mirror hanging in the Octagon room. On either side of the room is a conservatory.

Travels through North America, during the years 1825 and 1826 by His Highness Bernhard, Duke of Saxe-Weimar Eisenach, published in 1828, says of Sophia, Lady Edgcumbe:

We saw the monument of Lady Mount Edgcumbe, who died in 1806, to whom the park is indebted for most of its improvements. It is told of her that she was twice buried; the first time she remained three days in a vault, lying in her coffin, and was aroused by a thief cutting off her finger to steal a ring: she left the grave, took refuge in a neighbouring house, made herself known, and was re-conveyed to her castle, where she subsequently lived several years and gave birth to children.

The story about Lady Edgcumbe being revived by a thief is an interesting one. This seems to be an accurate tale that has been repeated many times as in *The Gentleman's Magazine* of 1853:

Another circumstance, far more extraordinary than any yet related in connection with Cotehele, is so well authenticated that not even a doubt rests about its truth, and with the relation of it this paper shall be brought to a close. It refers to the mother of Sir Richard Edgcumbe, knight, who, in 1748, was created Baron of Mount Edgcumbe.

The family were residing at Cotehele (I do not know the date or the year) when Lady Edgcumbe became much indisposed, and, to all appearance, died. How long after is not stated, but her body was deposited in the family vault of the parish church. The interment had not long taken place before the sexton (who must have heard from the nurse or the servants that she was buried with something of value upon her) went down into the vault at midnight, and contrived to force open the coffin. A gold ring was on her ladyship's finger, which, in a hurried way, he attempted to draw off, but not readily succeeding, he pressed with great violence the finger. Upon this the body moved in the coffin, and such was the terror of the man that he ran away as fast as he could, leaving his lantern behind him. Lady Edgcumbe arose, astonished at finding herself dressed in grave-clothes, and numbered with the tenants of the vault. She took up the lantern, and proceeded at once to the mansion of Cotehele. The terror, followed by the rejoicing of her family and household, which such a resurrection from the tomb occasioned may well be conceived. Exactly five years after this circumstance she became the mother of Sir Richard Edgcumbe who was created baron.

However, the mother of Sir Richard Edgcumbe was Lady Ann Montagu and not Sophia. Later versions of the story tell of the same events befalling Emma (1791–1872), the daughter of Richard, the 2nd Earl (1764–1839) and Lady Sophia Hobart (1768–1806) and this version has appeared in many books. Although the tale seems like it might be true, the exact details seem to have been muddled over the years.

Still on the Mount Edgcumbe estate, **Fern Dell**, also known as the Pets Cemetery, contains the graves of many of the Edgcumbe's dogs including Banjo who died in 1895, Louie who died in 1949 and Pepper who died in 1920. It is felt to be a gloomy place being set down from the other gardens in an old quarry pit and because of its many tall ferns and over-growing ivy.

As mentioned, the cemetery may have been the resting place of Cupid, the pig belonging to the Countess of Mount Edgcumbe. The pig accompanied her everywhere, much to the amusement of her friends. When it died, a Kingsbridge man wrote an ode to it which read:

Ode to the Countess of Mount Edgcumbe on the death of her pet pig Cupid:
Oh dry those tears so round and big,
Nor waste in sight your precious wind,
Death only takes a little pig
Your Lord and Son are still behind.

There was an urn dedicated to Cupid at Fern Dell but unfortunately, this monument has now been removed. On one of his visits to Mount Edgcumbe, George III, on reportedly seeing Cupid's headstone, remarked to Queen Charlotte, 'It's the family vault, Charley! The family vault!'

The area has been replanted with ivies and tree ferns in recent years and the seats and headstones have been repaired. Although a somewhat eerie and quiet place, it's interesting to visit and imagine the lives the pets had with their owners and the many well-known people of the day that visited the estate. The fountain features a face which seems suitable to the cold and eerie setting. Water, at one time, spouted from its mouth into the drinking trough below.

The **Blockhouse** on the estate is a Tudor fort which saw action during the Civil War. It was built in 1545 to defend the mouth of the Tamar and also to protect Stonehouse which lay opposite.

During the Civil War, Colonel Piers Edgcumbe (1610–1667) sided with the Royalists but, with the Parliamentarians occupying Plymouth, he wisely moved to Cotehele. Mount Edgcumbe was attacked several times by the Parliamentarian forces. A Lieutenant Colonel Martin attacked Mount Edgcumbe and captured three guns from the blockhouse before attacking Maker Church, which had been fortified by the Royalist garrison of Mount Edgcumbe. At the same time, Martin also captured the fort at Cawsand. In May 1644, Mount Edgcumbe was again attacked, this time by Captain Haynes. Outbuildings were set on fire and the Banqueting Hall was damaged. The Royalists of Edgcumbe refused to surrender but in the following year, Piers Edgcumbe surrendered to Sir Thomas Fairfax under the condition that he kept his family estate intact.

The Blockhouse became less used as a defence when the Battery was built on the shore in 1747 and then enlarged between 1862 and 1863. There is another Blockhouse still standing to this day which can be seen on the rocks opposite.

Barn Pool is a sheltered deep water area of Mount Edgcumbe. A large polished stone axe was found by divers near a reef at Barn Pool. The

This photo shows a mock battle put on to entertain the Royal visitors to Barn Pool in 1880. Ships that took part in the battle included the training brigs, Liberty Pilot *and* Nautilus.

area is likely to have been above sea-level during Neolithic times and was also used by the Vikings in 997. There is a shipwreck further offshore, the *Catharina von Flensburg*, which sank there in 1786.

Famous visitors who would have landed at Barn Pool include George III, Queen Charlotte and Princess Amelia who visited on 25 August 1789.

Charles Darwin's journey is mentioned in the *Quarterly Review* of 1840:

On the 27th November, 1831, the well-manned, well-appointed and well-provided Beagle *sailed from Barn Pool, and having circumnavigated the globe, and accomplished all the objects the expedition had in view, as far was practical, she anchored at Falmouth on the 2nd October, 1836, after an absence of four years and nine months.*

Darwin had lived in Plymouth for two months before his famous voyage around the world in HMS *Beagle*, captained by Robert Fitzroy. Darwin, who was then just 22 years old, joined the crew as a naturalist. He had a wealthy family who paid the £30 fare needed to travel on the *Beagle*.

Before leaving, he visited and walked the Mount Edgcumbe estate, and on various occasions visited Rame Head, Millbrook, Whitsand Bay and Cawsand which, he wrote in his journal of 17 December, 1831, was *'one of the most curiously built places I ever saw. It is situated in a very pretty little bay, which shelters numerous fishing and smuggling boats from the sea.'*

Barn Pool is also famous for being the area where American servicemen left for the D-Day invasion during 1944. The troops were stationed at Maker Camp. The deep anchorage by Barn Pool made it the ideal access point for military vehicles. A slipway was laid which consisted of a material known as chocolate box hards. Parts of these can still be seen today on the shoreline.

In June 1944, thousands of American troops left from here for the shores of Northern France.

The view down to Barn Pool towards the point where the Americans left for D-Day.

If you walk from Empacombe towards the Obelisk, there are several old disused buildings on the right. These were used by the US army as a fuel depot. On the shore, near to the depot, can still be seen the area where the pipes ran towards the water's edge where the River Tamar would have been full with American ships preparing for the D-Day landing on Utah Beach in Normandy. The pipes have been removed from the shore but still lie in a pile nearby over 70 years later. The buildings are mainly empty and some have graffiti on them. The building's original use during the war is probably long forgotten by many people.

During the Second World War much of the Mount Edgcumbe Estate was occupied by the War Department. This included the parkland adjoining Maker Church, the Garden Battery, Beechwood Cottages, the roads and drives and Barrow Park. The Admiralty requisitioned Barn Pool and the Amphitheatre, the Maker Fuel Depots, Obelisk Field, Cremyll, the tennis courts and electricity plant, the sheep park and the stables. A pipeline was installed at Lower Chapel Fields to fuel the ships for D-Day in 1944. This remained the property of the Admiralty until 1954. A report was made concerning the damage to the formal gardens between 1943 and 1947.

Some of the trees within the park still carry the names of the US servicemen who left from Barn Pool. These ones read, above, 'McCalip, 1944, Schott' and, below, 'J W 1944' and 'Earl R Lawton June, 1944.'

The Folly on the estate was built in 1747 and replaced the Obelisk which had stood on the site previously. It was built by using medieval stone from the churches of St George and St Lawrence which once stood in Stonehouse. The same stone was used to build the

The Folly at Mount Edgcumbe. Drake's Island and Plymouth can be seen in the background. The Folly was built in 1747 and replaced an Obelisk which had stood on the site previously. It was built by using medieval stone from the churches of St George and St Lawrence which once stood in Stonehouse.

A recent photo showing the Folly at Mount Edgcumbe. The Folly was known as 'The Ruins' for many years. Parts of the old Stonehouse Barrier Gates were also said to have been used in its construction. As Stonehouse was never a walled town, it is thought that these came from the Abbey or Manor House.

Picklecombe Seat further along the coast. Part of the seat features a medieval doorway. The church of St Lawrence was removed to make way for the Royal William Victualling Yard. The Folly was known as 'The Ruins' for many years. Parts of the old Stonehouse Barrier Gates were also said to have been used. As Stonehouse was never a walled town, it is thought that these came from the Abbey or Manor House.

Travelling further along by foot, the visitor arrives at **Picklecombe**. The original battery at Fort Picklecombe was built of earth in 1849. Between 1864 and 1871, a more substantial building replaced it made of granite with iron shields. It was armed with forty-two guns and was one of three main fortifications protecting the Sound.

Picklecombe Fort was commissioned by Lord Palmerston who was the foreign secretary and Prime Minister during the reign

Picklecombe Fort and the breakwater. Picklecombe Fort was commissioned by Lord Palmerston who was the foreign secretary and Prime Minister during the reign of Queen Victoria. Palmerston's forts appeared all over Britain following concerns over the size of the French Navy.

of Queen Victoria. Palmerston's forts appeared all over Britain following concerns over the size of the French Navy. They gained the name, Palmerston's Follies and by the time they were completed, the threat had passed. They were said to be the most expensive system of defence structures ever built in Britain during times of peace.

The 1881 census shows Fort Picklecombe occupied by the military and their families. Residents at the time included one major, four sergeants, three corporals, five bombers, two trumpeters, fifty-seven gunners as well as several wives and children.

Fort Picklecombe was redeveloped into apartments in the 1970s and is now a private establishment. Unfortunately, the area is no longer open to the general public. The fort is an interesting feature but isn't as easily accessible as it once was although it's an important part of the area's history.

In 1483, a handful of fishermen lived at **Kingsand** and **Cawsand** when Henry VII landed in an abortive attempt to try to overthrow Richard III.

The population grew when Plymouth merchants built pilchard cellars along the shore in the time of Elizabeth I. For the next two centuries, smuggling also flourished.

In 1844 the pilchard fishery in both Kingsand and Cawsand employed fifty men.

Up until 1844, Kingsand was in Devon and a boundary marker between the two counties can still be seen opposite the Halfway Hotel which separated Turk Town (Cawsand) and North Rockers (Kingsand).

Horatio Nelson was said to have visited the village and to have dined at the Ship Inn. Famous residents have included Ann Davison who sailed the Atlantic single-handed in 1953. Arthur Ransome's daughter Tabitha also lived here. Ransome was famous for writing *Swallows and Amazons.*

Daytrippers at Kingsand in the early 1900s. Up until 1844, Kingsand was still in Devon and a boundary marker between the two counties can still be seen opposite the Halfway Hotel which separated Turk Town (Cawsand) and North Rockers (Kingsand).

The History of Cornwall by Fortescue Hitchins and Samuel Drew, published in 1824, stated:

Trending Penlee Point,' says Carew, 'you discover Kingsand and Cawsand Bay, an open road, yet sometimes affording succour to the worst of seafarers, as not subject to the controlment of Plymouth forts. The shore is peopled with some dwelling-houses and many cellars, dearly rented for a short usage in saving pilchards; at which time there flocketh a great number of seiners and others depending on their labour. I have heard the inhabitants thereabout report, that the Earl of Richmond, afterwards Henry VII, while he hovered upon the coast, here by stealth refreshed himself; but being advertised of strait watch kept for him at Plymouth, he richly rewarded his host, hied speedily on shipboard, and escaped happily to a better fortune.

In 1597, a Spanish ship coming into the bay, while most of the active men were absent at an assize, seized this favourable opportunity to send a party on shore in the dead of night to make preparations for setting the town on fire. To accomplish this, they hung up some barrels of combustible matter to several doors, to which a train was set, that at a given time should take fire, and execute their purpose. Happily however, the design being discovered before the explosion took place, these unwelcome guests were removed, and the Spaniards driven on board their ship. Carew observes, that the contriver of this plot was a Portuguese, who had sailed with Sir John Boroughs, and boasted to have burned his ship. For these two honourable exploits the king of Spain is said to have rewarded him with 200 ducats.

Kingsand and Cawsand contain many houses and many inhabitants. About forty years since, smuggling was carried on here to a considerable extent; at which time this place produced some of the most able seamen in the west of England. But of late years, since this contraband traffic has been on the decline, the inhabitants have directed their talents into another channel. Some branches of the Royal Navy riding in this bay during the late war, furnished the industrious with employment in trading to the ships, and supplying their crews with necessaries. This consolidated town lies in a pleasant vale on the margin of the tide. It has many well-built houses; and from those situated on elevated ground, the prospects are extensive, diversified and pleasing. The streets however, are narrow and irregular, and cannot be distinguished for the excellence of their pavement, or extraordinary cleanliness.

The small village of **Cawsand** proved to be perfectly placed for the practice of smuggling. Goods from France such as tobacco, tea and rum were off loaded from incoming ships and taken to shore by longshoremen's boats. Open boats, normally used for seine-net fishing to catch pilchards were manned by six-man crews and were well adapted to meet ships to offload goods. They were also able to cross the Channel in these boats and could carry as much as six tons of brandy at a time. Larger boats could carry as much as 800 eight-gallon spirit casks as well as sundry other goods. In 1804, the collector of Customs in Plymouth estimated that over 17,000 casks of wine were smuggled into Cawsand and avoided duty every year. In 1815, fifty boats were involved in the trade.

There were many battles between smugglers and revenue men within the bay. In one, in 1788, Henry Carter, who was one of Cornwall's most famous smugglers and who was nicknamed the 'King of Prussia', barely escaped with his life, though he lost his cutter in the fight. Henry Carter's real name was John Carter and he modelled himself on Frederick the Great, the King of Prussia. Carter lived at what is known today as Prussia Cove, originally

An early view of the village at Cawsand, complete with horse and buggy. The small village proved to be perfectly placed for the practice of smuggling. Goods from France such as tobacco, tea and rum were off loaded from incoming ships and taken to shore by longshoremen's boats.

Porthleah, in West Cornwall and the name has been adopted from his nickname.

When the smuggling trade finally ended, Cawsand men returned to fishing and pilotage.

A young sailor from Cawsand, Lieutenant John Pollard, was a midshipman on the *Victory* when Admiral Lord Nelson was fatally wounded. Although not a well-known name now, it was Pollard who shot and killed the enemy sailor who shot Nelson. He was known thereafter as, 'Nelson's Avenger'. However, several other men also claimed to have shot the Frenchman.

In *An Authentic Narrative of the Death of Lord Nelson* by Sir William Beatty, published in 1807, he wrote:

> *There were only two Frenchmen left alive in the mizzen-top of the* Redoubtable *at the time of his Lordship's being wounded and by the hands of these he fell. At length one of them was killed by a musket ball; and on the others then attempting to make his escape from the top down the rigging, Mr Pollard (Midshipman) fired his musket at him and shot him in the back when he fell dead from the shrouds on the* Redoutable's *poop.'*

Beatty was the Ship's Surgeon on HMS *Victory* and his account supports Pollard as being the 'avenger'.

Captain Frederick Lewis Maitland sailed from Cawsand Bay on 24 May, 1815, in command of His Majesty's ship, *Bellerophon*. Napoleon was defeated at the Battle of Waterloo on 18 June 1815. With the French army in disarray, coalition forces were able to enter France and restore Louis XVIII to the French throne. Unable to return to France, Napoleon made his way towards America. Maitland intercepted Napoleon at Rochefort and after negotiations, Napoleon surrendered to Maitland on 15 July 1815.

Maitland refused Napoleon passage to America and took him to England, arriving at Torbay on 24 July where he was ordered to proceed to Plymouth. Napoleon was to spend the last six years of his life in exile, under British supervision, on the island of St Helena.

Nettleton's Guide of 1829 described Cawsand and Kingsand within its pages:

> *This place has partaken largely in the prosperity which the whole neighbourhood owes to the naval establishments in the district. In Carew's time, it consisted of only a few fisherman's huts; it now contains over 300 houses, many of them large and well-built. Its support which, in time of war, was principally derived from the number of ships which resorted to the bay, is now confined to the fisheries, particularly that of pilchards which we regret have been unproductive for many years past. Two dissenting places of worship are well attended by the inhabitants, the respective churches being at a considerable distance. On a rocky eminence which arises near the centre of Cawsand are the vestiges of a fortification at present called 'The Bulwarks'.*
>
> *During the tremendous storm of 1817, this town sustained very great injury. Some houses on the beach were entirely destroyed by the violence of the waters and there was property lost and destroyed to a considerable amount. It also suffered in the hurricane of November 1824 and January 1828 when the destruction again was very extensive.*

On 28 April 1912, the *Titanic* survivors were brought back to Millbay Docks, fourteen days after the ship sank. At 8am, the SS *Lapland* moored at Cawsand Bay with the 167 members of the *Titanic* who hadn't been detained in New York for the American inquiry. Three tenders left Millbay Docks to collect the passengers and the 1,927 sacks of mail that had been scheduled to be carried by the *Titanic*. The third tender, the *Sir Richard Grenville*, carrying the survivors, killed time in the Sound while the dock labourers and

The church at Maker. In the Domesday Book of 1086, Maker was held by Reginald from Robert, Count of Mortain. The value of the manor, at the time, was £1.

Penlee Point. In 1871, a beacon stood at Penlee Point, a lofty obelisk which was used by sailors as a landmark.

porters were paid off and escorted out of the dock gates at West Hoe. After midday, the tender was given the all clear and the survivors were allowed to disembark in an air of secrecy. They were then put on a special train from Millbay Docks to Southampton where they arrived at 10.10pm that night.

Maker lies above Kingsand; its name in Cornish means 'ruin'. During Norman times, the Valletorts owned much of the land bordering the River Tamar. However, Maker then passed on to the Durnford family, by marriage, before then being owned by the Edgcumbes.

In the Domesday Book of 1086, Maker was held by Reginald from Robert, Count of Mortain. The value of the manor, at the time, was £1. The church of St Julian was built in the fifteenth century. The font within the church is Norman, but was originally located at St Merryn. In 1874, the Edgcumbe part of the chapel was built. The barrister and writer, William Hughes, was born in Maker.

Following the coast towards Rame Head, the visitor comes to **Penlee Point.** Duprez's Guide of 1871 states: *'At Penlee Point is the Beacon, a lofty obelisk erected as a landmark for sailors. Here is also a pretty Gothic building called 'Adelaide's Chapel' in honour of the Queen, who during a visit in 1827 made many excursions to the spot.'* The Beacon mentioned was said to be a Folly Tower which stood above the ridge of Queen Adelaide's Chapel. It was erected by the first Earl so that he could signal to his returning ships. It was considered a security risk and removed during the First World War. Queen Adelaide (1792–1849) was the wife of William IV (1765–1837). Adelaide in Australia was named after her in 1836. Queen Adelaide's Grotto was originally just a cave and was used as a watch house in the eightenth century. It was enhanced with an arched stone frontage and became a grotto after Adelaide's visit in 1827. If you didn't know it was there, it would be easy to miss as it is set down from the main walking path above.

At **Rame Head**, hermits lived at the ancient chapel of St Michael and kept a light burning to warn ships of the danger of the nearby

Queen Adelaide's Grotto at Penlee Point as it is today. It was originally just a cave and was used as a watch house in the eighteenth century. It was enhanced with an arched stone frontage and became a grotto after Adelaide's visit in 1827.

Rame Head. Hermits once lived at the ancient chapel of St Michael and kept a light burning to warn ships of the danger of the nearby rocks. The first record of the chapel appears in 1397.

rocks. The first record of the chapel appears in 1397. By 1425, a licence was granted to hold mass every Monday and at Michaelmas.

By 1488 the men who inhabited the chapel were paid 4d for 'keeping of ye bekying'. They would also report back any news of incoming vessels. In 1588, two watchmen were paid to keep a look out for Spanish vessels after the abortive attempt of the Armada. During the First World War, an anti-submarine gun was mounted on

A father and his daughter enjoying the sun at the Grotto at Freathy Beach, Whitsands. The small cave was dug out by hand by a hermit called Lugger in 1874. Inside, he chipped out verses on the ceiling.

Victorian daytrippers enjoying the beach at Whitsands. On 16 January 1914, HMS A7, an early type of Royal Navy submarine, sank in Whitsand Bay. The crew, who were carrying out dummy torpedo attacks, were all lost.

a platform near the chapel and in the Second World War, a concrete gun platform was built and a mobile radar station was located there.

St Michael the Archangel is known as the patron saint of high and exposed places such as St Michael's Mount in Marazion and Mont-Saint-Michel, in Normandy.

Flint tools found in the area date from the Mesolithic period. In the Iron Age, the headland was separated from the mainland by a huge ditch.

In 1882, the chapel was restored by William, the 4th Earl of Edgcumbe.

Whitsand Bay stretches along the coast from Rame Head in the east towards Portwrinkle in the west. It includes **Polhawn Cove, Freathy** and **Tregonhawke**. At **Sharrow Point**, there is a small cave which was dug out by hand by a hermit called Lugger in 1874. Inside, he chipped out verses on the ceiling.

On 16 January 1914, HMS *A7*, an early type of Royal Navy submarine, sank in Whitsand Bay. The crew, who were carrying out dummy torpedo attacks, were all lost. Attempts to salvage the vessel were made but all failed and the wreck remains where she sank over 100 years ago.

A photo from the early 1900s showing children enjoying donkey rides on the beach at Freathy. Most were probably daytrippers from nearby Plymouth.

The beach at Tregantle. Tregantle Fort was completed in 1865. Originally, it had accomodation for 1,000 men. In the early 1900s, it was an infantry battalion headquarters and housed 14 officers and 423 other ranks.

Two Palmerston forts lie on the coast. **Polhawn Battery** was built between 1862 and 1867. During the First World War, the battery was used for accommodation. In 1927, it was sold off and today, it's used as a hotel and wedding venue.

Tregantle Fort was completed in 1865. Originally, it had accommodation for 1,000 men. In the early 1900s, it was an infantry battalion headquarters and housed 14 officers and 423 other ranks. From 1903, it was used for rifle training.

After the First World War, the fort lay empty until the beginning of the Second World War, when it was used as the Territorial Army Passive Air Defence School. During the war, the fort was used as the Army Gas School before being used as accommodation for American troops in 1942. Since the end of the war, it has been used by the army and also by the Royal Marines for training.

Further along the coast is **Crafthole**, a small village, which, in the 1800s, was notorious for smuggling rum. The rum was

The beach at Downderry. Off the coast of Downderry lies the wreck of the Gipsy. *It was formerly known as* The Rodney *and was an iron full-rigged ship built in 1874 by W. Pile & Co. of Sunderland.*

offloaded at the harbour at **Portwrinkle** before being taken uphill to Crafthole. Much of the rum was stored in a room below the Methodist Chapel.

Portwrinkle was once a small fishing village. The walls of the seventeenth century pilchard cellars still stand although, today, now incorporate housing.

Further along the coast are the small villages of **Downderry** and **Seaton**. From the villages, out to sea, can be seen Looe Island to the west and Rame Head to the east. Eddystone Lighthouse lies 8 miles out and can be seen on clear days. Nearby Triffle Farm has the only known example of a 'cursus' earthwork in Cornwall.

Off the coast of Downderry lies the wreck of the *Gipsy*. It was formerly known as *The Rodney* and was an iron full-rigged ship built in 1874 by W. Pile & Co. of Sunderland. During November, the Rodney lost her figurehead in a storm in the English Channel. It turned up six months later at Whitsand Bay. In 1897, the vessel was sold to F. Boissière, of Nantes, France, renamed Gipsy and re-tigged as a barque. The ship was wrecked on 7 December 1901, on the return voyage from Iquique (Chile) to France while carrying a cargo of nitrate. The vessel was later blown up by explosives after she had become a hazard to local fishing vessels.

The Church of St Nicholas in Downderry dates from the late nineteenth century.

A Chain Home radar installation was located in Downderry during the Second World War. Its remains can be found on the east side of the village. One of the bunkers in now a residential garage.

The road from Seaton, following the coast, eventually leads to **Looe**.

CHAPTER 3

St Austell to Falmouth

St Austell, 10 miles south of Bodmin, is one of the largest towns in Cornwall. It is named after Saint Austol, a sixth-century Cornish holy man who spent most of his life in Brittany.

Soon after William Cookworthy discovered china clay at Tregonning hill in west Cornwall, an even greater quantity was discovered in Hensbarrow downs, just north of St Austell.

The excavation of clay took over from tin and copper mining and became the principal industry in the area. This led to a great expansion of the town as the trade took off in the mid-nineteenth to early twentieth century. Falling prices of tin and other metals meant

An early view of the church and Church Street, St Austell. The town is named after Saint Austol, a sixth-century Cornish holy man who spent most of his life in Brittany.

that many mines had to close and many workers found jobs within the town, excavating clay, which increased the population greatly. Eventually, St Austell became one of the major commercial centres in Cornwall. Redevelopment in the town began in 1963 when a pedestrian precinct together with shops, offices and flats was built.

Mevagissey lies 5 miles south of St Austell. The village incorporates a fishing port and lies in a small valley which faces east towards Mevagissey Bay. Tourism is one of the village's main sources of income although fishing, on a smaller scale, still takes place. The harbour is also the home to many pleasure boats.

Mevagissey first appears in records in 1313 when it was known as Porthhilly. Evidence has been discovered suggesting that there was once a Bronze Age settlement in the area.

The parish was originally known as Lamorrick and formed part of the episcopal manor of Tregear. In 1259 the church was dedicated by Bishop Bronescombe to Saints Meva and Ida. By 1329 Sir Otho

The small fishing village at Mevagissey. The village first appears in records in 1313 when it was known as Porthhilly.

Bodrugan appropriated it to Glasney College. In the fifteenth century, the Norman church was much rebuilt. During the Commonwealth period, the tower fell into disrepair and the bells were sold to a Quaker living at St Austell. It is said that a church has stood on the same site since 500AD.

There are three holy wells in Mevagissey. Both the Brass Well and Lady's Well lie within the manor of Treleaven; the third holy well is at the old vicarage within the grounds of Mevagissey House.

At the end of the 1600s, Porthhilly joined the hamlet of Lamoreck and became a new village. Originally, the village was called 'Meva hag Ysi', named after two Irish saints, St Meva and St Issey.

The village gained its income from pilchard fishing and smuggling. At the time, there were at least ten inns located there. Of these two remain: the Fountain and the Ship.

In 1768, the founder of Pears' Soap, Andrew Pears, was born in Mevagissey where he set up a barber's shop, which he ran until he moved to London in 1789.

St Mawes is located opposite Falmouth on the Roseland peninsula. It was once a very busy fishing port but today prospers more due to the tourism trade. The town lies on the east bank of the Carrick Roads which is a large flooded valley created soon after the Ice Age. The melt waters caused the sea to rise dramatically which created a natural harbour. A ferry takes passengers to and from Falmouth, a quicker journey than by road.

The town's name is derived from the Celtic saint, Saint Maudez (Mawe).

St Mawes was made a borough in 1563 and at the time returned two members to parliament. In 1832 it was disenfranchised. In 1880 it was described as a small fishing village with one main street, a pier, sea-wall and a parapet. The pier had been built in 1854.

St Mawes Castle was built in the time of Henry VIII to repel any future French attacks. The coastal fortress is still well-preserved.

The castle at St Mawes which was built in the time of Henry VIII to repel any future French attacks. The coastal fortress is still well-preserved.

The harbour at St Mawes. The town lies on the east bank of the Carrick Roads which is a large flooded valley created soon after the Ice Age.

Penryn lies one mile north-west of Falmouth and is situated on the Penryn River. It is one of Cornwall's most ancient towns and first appears in the Domesday Book, when it was called 'Trelivel'. The Bishop of Exeter named the town Penryn in 1216. A religious college, known as Glasney College, was built in 1265. During 1374, the chapel of St Thomas was opened.

At the mouth of Penryn River, the port lies in a sheltered location and during the fifteenth century, played a significant role. In 1548 Glasney College was dissolved and knocked down in the reign of Edward VI who was the first Protestant Duke of Cornwall and later the king of England. In 1549 the dissolution of the college led to the Prayer Book Rebellion which was later defeated.

In 1621 Penryn obtained a royal charter as a borough with the hope that this would lead to the end of piracy in the area. Between 1550 and 1650, three mayors of the town were convicted of piracy. By the mid 1600s the port had become prosperous through its fishing, tin and copper trade.

The town supported the Parliamentary side during the English Civil War of 1642 to 1648 and this led to it losing both its custom house and market rights to Falmouth. The town continued to decline as Falmouth grew. However, in the early nineteenth century granite works were established by the river and large quantities of the stone were shipped from its quays for construction projects both within the UK and abroad.

Falmouth lies on the River Fal. In 1540, Henry VIII had Pendennis Castle built to help defend Carrick Roads. In 1613, Sir John Killigrew created the town of Falmouth which took over much of the prosperity once enjoyed by nearby Penryn.

Angled ramparts were added to the defences at Pendennis in the sixteenth century when there was a threat of an attack by the Spanish Armada. During the English Civil War, Pendennis Castle was captured by the Parliamentary Army and was the second to last

A busy scene in High Street, Falmouth. In 1613 Sir John Killigrew created the town which took much of the prosperity once enjoyed by nearby Penryn.

Falmouth from the gardens. From 1689 until 1851, the Falmouth Packet Service operated from Falmouth carrying mail to and from Britain's ever expanding empire.

fort to surrender. Sir Peter Killigrew was granted royal patronage after the Civil War after building a church which he dedicated to King Charles I.

From 1689 until 1851, the Falmouth Packet Service operated from Falmouth carrying mail to and from Britain's ever expanding empire. As the most south-westerly harbour in Great Britain, Falmouth was often the first place that Royal Navy ships docked when returning from overseas.

CHAPTER 4

Truro

The city of **Truro** was originally a centre for trade and a stannary town involved in the tin mining industry.

The first recorded settlement in the area was during Norman times. Richard de Luci built a castle there in the twelfth century and the town grew up close by. Today, the castle no longer exists. De Luci was the Chief Justice of England during the reign of Henry II, and was granted land in Cornwall for his service to the crown.

Lemon Street, Truro. Stylish Georgian and Victorian townhouses were constructed in the eighteenth and nineteenth centuries to house the wealthy and some of these can be found in Lemon Street.

In 1138, after leaving Falaise, Richard de Luci fought in Cornwall under the command of Count Alan of Brittany. The castle built by de Luci later passed to Reginald FitzRoy, the illegitimate son of Henry I. Fitzroy became the first earl of Cornwall after being invested by King Stephen. By 1270 the castle was little more than a ruin and it was levelled in 1840. The Crown Court stands on the site today. By the beginning of the 1300s, Truro had become a major port, partly because its inland position sheltered it from invaders. It prospered from fishing and became one of Cornwall's stannary towns for assayed and stamped tin and copper dug from Cornish mines.

Much of the population left during the time of the Black Death and this, together with a trade recession, resulted in the town becoming much neglected. During the Tudor period the town grew again and in 1589, self-governance was awarded by a charter granted by Elizabeth I. This gave Truro an elected mayor and control over the port of Falmouth.

Truro supported the king during the English Civil War in the 1600s and a royalist mint was set up in the area. When Parliamentary troops arrived in 1646, the mint was relocated in Exeter.

In the later 1600s, Falmouth was given charter rights meaning that it had control of its own harbour. This led to a rivalry between Falmouth and Truro. In 1709 the dispute was resolved when both towns gained a divided control of the River Fal.

Truro grew in prosperity during the eighteenth and nineteenth centuries. Better mining methods meant that industry flourished and tin sold for higher prices which attracted well-off mine owners to the town. Stylish Georgian and Victorian townhouses were constructed to house the wealthy and some of these can be found in Lemon Street. The street was named after the MP, Sir William Lemon, a mining entrepreneur. At one time, Truro was known as 'the London of Cornwall' and attracted high society to the county.

During the same time, Truro remained prosperous and had many famous residents including Richard Lander, the explorer, who found

Boscawen Street, Truro in the 1920s. Truro supported the king during the English Civil War in the 1600s and a royalist mint was set up in the area. When Parliamentary troops arrived in 1646, the mint was relocated in Exeter.

the mouth of the River Niger in Africa. He was awarded the first gold medal by the Royal Geographical Society for his achievement. Henry Martyn also lived in Truro and went on to read mathematics at Cambridge before being ordained and becoming a missionary. He later translated the New Testament into Urdu and Persian.

Humphry Davy was educated in Truro and became the inventor of the miner's safety lamp. Samuel Foote, both an actor and playwright, hailed from Boscawen Street.

In the late nineteenth century, Truro grew and had its own smelting works, potteries and tanneries making it the most prominent Cornish town. In the 1860s the Great Western Railway arrived and linked the town with London. In 1876, the Bishopric of Truro Act gave the town first a bishop, followed by its own cathedral. The town was granted city status by Queen Victoria in 1877.

As the city entered the twentieth century, there was a decline in the mining industry but Truro still remained prosperous as it became the commercial centre of Cornwall and developed greatly.

CHAPTER 5

St Keverne to Porthleven

St Keverne lies on the Lizard Peninsula. People have inhabited the area for thousands of years and artefacts found date back to the Mesolithic period, approximately 5,550BC. The surrounding area is abundant in archaeological history including flints, pottery, cists, round houses and cliff castles. During Neolithic times and afterwards, St Keverne became one of the major sources of clay for pottery. Over an area of approximately 7 square miles along the Lizard Peninsula, at a depth of 8 to 18 inches below the topsoil, lies Gabbroic clay from which much of the Palaeolithic pottery found in Cornwall is made, including the sherds at the Neolithic site of Carn Brea at Redruth.

The small village of St Keverne. People have inhabited the area for thousands of years and artefacts found date back to the Mesolithic period, approximately 5,550BC.

The village has yielded a huge quantity of Beaker pottery, while the Beaker Mound, located at Poldowrian, has produced one of the best caches of Beaker pottery within the county.

At Goonhilly Downs, there are over 65 Bronze Age barrows. Also located in the area is the 'dry tree' standing stone. At Tremenheere, there is a further Bronze Age standing stone. Tremenheere translates to 'Standing Stone Farm', from 'Tre' meaning place or farm and 'Menhir' meaning standing stone. At Ludgvan, another place also carries the same name. On Crowza Downs, there is a cist which is named the Three Brothers of Grugith and at Polkernogo, there is a destroyed fogou, an underground dry-stone structure.

There are a number of Iron Age sites within the village. These include the one time dramatic cliff castles of Chynalls and Lankidden. Little is left at these sites apart from faint markings where the ditches and banks that would have protected these castles ran. When the castles were in use, the area would have been densely populated with settlements of the time, known as 'rounds'.

In 1833, an elaborately engraved bronze mirror was discovered in a cist grave. It was found with two brooches, several beads and two rings.

In Celtic times, the village was part of the Meneage which was owned by several small monasteries. The monastery at St Keverne still stood after the Norman Conquest, however, it was seized shortly after by a lay lord.

By 1236 the churches and demesnes belonged to the Cistercian abbey at Beaulieu. In 1258 their title was confirmed by Earl Richard. This proved to be a valuable possession as it included the rectorial tithe of the large and prosperous parish, as well as the tithe of fish and the lands of the churchtown.

The right of sanctuary was given to St Keverne which was also held by Beaulieu Abbey. Monks worshipped at Tregonan and the remains of a building there were still in place in the early twentieth century.

In 1497 the Cornish Rebellion started in the village led by Michael An Gof who worked as a blacksmith in St Keverne. A statue of him stands within the village. He was caught and executed, but before he died, he said that he would have 'a name perpetual and a fame permanent and immortal'.

An important monastery stood in St Keverne during the Middle Ages. The large village church is dedicated to St Akeveranus and dates from the fifteenth century although it includes stone taken from a previous church building. A 32-pounder carronade which was recovered from the wreck of HMS *Primose* has been placed by the lych-gate on entry to the churchyard. On 21 January 1809, *Primrose* was destroyed near The Manacles just off The Lizard. Altogether, 125 people lost their lives but there was one survivor, a drummer boy.

During 1967, close to the Lankidden Cliff Castle, a Mesolithic site, known as Rock Mound, was discovered at Poldowrian Site. From hazelnut fragments, the site was dated to between 5,550 and 5,250BC. While ploughing the land, flint tools were first found. Once excavated, nearly 48,000 tools were discovered.

The Lizard forms part of the peninsula running along southern Cornwall. Lizard village is the most southerly village located on the British mainland and lies in the civil parish of Landewednack. The coast there has proved extremely hazardous in the past and the area was once known as 'the Graveyard of Ships'. In 1752 the Lizard Lighthouse was built at Lizard Point.

The name 'Lizard' is thought to be a corruption of the Cornish name 'Lys Ardh' which means 'high court'. Several burial mounds and stones lie nearby point to early habitation in the area. A part of the peninsula is known as the Meneage which means 'land of the monks'.

The closest town to the Lizard Peninsula is Helston which once headed the estuary of the River Cober. In the thirteenth century, Loe Bar cut this off from the sea. However, the bar was formed much earlier during the Ice Age. From 1260 onwards, the medieval port of Helston was found at Gweek on the Helford river. From here, tin and copper was exported. Helston has existed since the sixth century. The Domesday Book refers to the area as Henliston. In 1201, the town

The Lighthouse on the Lizard. The coast there has proved extremely hazardous in the past and the area was once known as 'the Graveyard of Ships'. In 1752, the Lizard Lighthouse was built at Lizard Point.

was granted a charter by King John. Tin ingots were weighed here to access the duty owed to the Duke of Cornwall.

At the time of the Domesday Book in 1086, the royal manor of Winnianton was held by King William I. It was the main manor of the hundred of Kerrier and the biggest estate in Cornwall.

On 29 July 1588, the first sighting of the Spanish Armada from the mainland was from Lizard Point. The Armada included 120 ships with 29,000 men with over 1,000 cannon on board. They were seen off by Lord Howard of Effingham, together with Sir Francis Drake as his Vice Admiral, and the force of the English fleet.

There have been many maritime disasters off the Lizard including those off the Manacles, a hazardous area of jagged rocks just beneath the sea. In 1619 the first light was put here built and paid for by

A view of the Lizard showing the lighthouse on the headland. The name 'Lizard' is thought to be a corruption of the Cornish name 'Lys Ardh' which means 'high court'.

Sir John Killigrew, said to be at a cost of '20 nobles a year' for thirty years. This caused such a fuss over the following years that King James I wanted to charge vessels to pass the point. The ensuing problems led to the lighthouse being demolished, however, it was rebuilt in 1751 by order of Thomas Fonnereau.

On 21 October 1707 during the War of the Spanish Succession the Battle at the Lizard, took place off the point. In 1721, the *Royal Anne* galley was wrecked off Lizard Point with only three people surviving out of a crew of 185. One of those lost was Lord Belhaven who was making his way overseas to take up the post of Governorship of Barbados.

In 1791 the Reverend William Gregor discovered titanium in the area.

Smuggling proved to be a popular and prosperous local pastime. In 1801, smugglers were offered the king's pardon if they gave any information concerning the Mullion musket men who had been involved in a gunfight with the crew of HM Gun Vessel *Hecate*.

In 1807 HMS *Anson*, a 44-gun frigate, was wrecked at Loe Bar. Many lost their lives even though the wreck took place close to shore. Henry Trengrouse invented the rocket-fired line because of this tragedy and undoubtedly saved countless lives. This would later become the Breeches buoy.

In 1809 *Dispatch*, a transport ship, ran aground on the Manacles. It was returning from the Peninsular War. A total of 104 men were lost, all from the 7th Hussars. The next day, while local villagers were still attempting a rescue, HMS *Primrose*, a Cruizer-class brig-sloop, hit the northern end of the rocks killing most on board.

During 1869, the Falmouth Gibraltar and Malta Telegraph company was formed by John Pender with the intention of connecting England to India using a cable running under the sea. Its landing point was at Porthcurno near Land's End.

In 1898, the SS *Mohegan*, a 7,000 tonne passenger liner, also hit the Manacles and 106 lost their lives. The following year, the American passenger liner, the *Paris*, became stranded on the Manacles but luckily, there was no loss of life.

In 1900 Guglielmo Marconi lodged at the Housel Bay Hotel while searching for a coastal radio station which could receive signals from ships equipped with his apparatus. He leased a plot in the wheat field adjoining the hotel and the Lizard Wireless Telegraph Station was constructed which still stands today. It is the oldest Marconi station to still exist in its original condition. The first trans Atlantic wireless signal radio communication was sent from Poldhu Point on 12 December 1901. From here, Marconi sent a signal to St John's in Newfoundland. The technology used led to the development of radio, television, satellites and the internet.

On 17 March 1907, the SS *Suevic*, a 12,000-tonne liner, hit the Maenheere Reef near Lizard Point. RNLI lifeboat volunteers, in poor weather conditions, managed to rescue 456 passengers including 70 babies. For sixteen hours, crews from the Lizard, Cadgwith, Coverack and Porthleven rowed out to rescue those on board.

During the First World War, a Naval Air Station was built at Bonython. This flew mainly blimps which were used to spot U-boats. One U-boat was sunk by a bomb dropped from a blimp and several others were damaged.

Anti-submarine sorties were flown from RAF Predannack Down during the Second World War. They also offered convoy support in the western English Channel. RAF Drytree, a radar station, was also constructed in the area. In 1962 the location was used in connection with the Telstar project and later became the Goonhilly satellite earth station.

The novelist Daphne du Maurier based many of her stories on this part of Cornwall, including *Frenchman's Creek*.

The area is well known for its carved serpentine items, which include various ornaments, as well as the pump handles in the local public house, the Lizard Inn (The Top House).

Mullion is a small village on the Lizard Peninsula approximately 5 miles north of Helston. Prehistoric burial mounds, Celtic crosses and ancient chapel sites can be found in the area and, in recent times, copper and china clay was mined there. At Angrowse several barrows were excavated which yielded prehistoric remains. A Cornish cross lies close to the hamlet of Predannack.

The rocky shores at Mullion Cove. Prehistoric burial mounds, Celtic crosses and ancient chapel sites can be found in the area and, in recent times, copper and China clay was mined there.

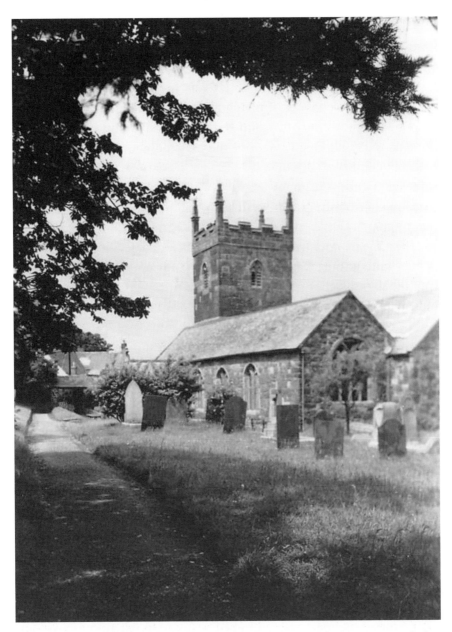

The church at Mullion. The chancel of the church was rebuilt some time before 1331 by the executors of Bishop Bytton of Exeter. Part of the chancel remains today although much of the existing church dates from the fifteenth century.

A Celtic church is thought to have existed in the area. In Norman times, it lay in the fief of Rosewick. In 1291 John de Rivers gifted the church to Mottesfont Priory, however, in 1309 the priory conveyed it to the Dean and Chapter of Exeter. In 1310 the vicarage was established. The chancel of the church was rebuilt some time before 1331 by the executors of Bishop Bytton of Exeter. Part of the chancel remains today although much of the existing church dates from the fifteenth century.

In the 1700s, like many other Cornish villages, Mullion thrived from pilchard fishing. The fish were caught with a seine net and the pilchards were cured at Newlyn before being exported to Mediterranean countries where they were considered a delicacy. A huer (a look-out) was posted on Mullion Island and his job was to spot the dark patches of nearby shoals of pilchards. A small shellfish industry also operated in the area.

From as early as the middle 1700s there are records of copper mines in the area, however, the trade was short lived. The mine buildings have all gone but an adit remains in Mullion Cove.

At Soapy Cove, talc was quarried during the eighteenth century. The talc, which occurs as a vein in the serpentine, was used for early porcelain production by Benjamin Lund of Bristol and later by the Worcester Porcelain Manufacturers in 1752.

From 1867, the Royal National Lifeboat Institution moored a lifeboat at Mullion Cove and this continued until 1908.

In the six years leading up to 1873, there were nine wrecks along the $1\frac{1}{2}$ mile stretch of coastline beneath Mullion cliffs. Altogether, sixty-nine people lost their lives.

Porthleven is a town and fishing port close to Helston. It is the most southerly port in the UK and was originally a harbour for refuge as the surrounding coast was a blight for shipping where many vessels were wrecked. Before 1844, Porthleven fell within the parish of Sithney.

The harbour at Porthleven. Porthleven's most recognisable building, the Bickford-Smith Institute, complete with its 70ft tower, was built in 1883. The building was constructed by William Bickford-Smith who was an English fuse manufacturer.

It is assumed that the name Porthleven is connected with St Elwen or Elwyn. Before 1270, a chapel dedicated to him stood in the area. It was rebuilt in 1510 but was destroyed in 1549. At one time, there were also chapels at Higher Penrose and Lanner Veor as well as a holy well at Venton-Vedna.

Porthleven's parish church is dedicated to St Bartholomew and was constructed in 1842.

In 1863, the Royal National Lifeboat Institution stationed a lifeboat at Porthleven. A boat house was constructed at Breageside and in 1894 a new boat house was opened to the west side of the harbour entrance. This came complete with a slipway to make launching the boat much easier. Eventually, the station was closed in 1929.

Porthleven's most recognisable building, the Bickford-Smith Institute, complete with its 70ft tower, was built in 1883. The building was constructed by William Bickford-Smith, an English fuse manufacturer. He was also a Liberal and Liberal Unionist politician who sat in the House of Commons from 1885 to 1892.

CHAPTER 6

Helston to St Ives

Helston lies at the northern end of the Lizard Peninsula, approximately 12 miles east of Penzance. The name was originally 'hen lis' which is Cornish for 'old court'. The 'ton' part of the name denotes a Saxon manor. There is reference in the Domesday Book to 'Henliston'.

On 15 April 1201 King John granted the town its charter for forty marks of silver. Tin ingots were weighed at Helston to work out the tin coinage duty due to the Duke of Cornwall. The manor of Helston

An early street scene in Helston. On 15 April 1201, King John granted the town its charter for forty marks of silver. Tin ingots were weighed at Helston to work out the tin coinage duty due to the Duke of Cornwall.

The Furry Dance taking place at Helston. Flora Day takes place annually in the town on 8 May, except when the date falls on a Sunday or Monday. Monday is Helston's Market Day.

was originally one of the seventeen Antiqua maneria (ancient manors) of the Duchy of Cornwall. It has been said that Helston was once a port although no records exist.

A castle once stood in the town built before 1086 as a motte and bailey structure. At the time it was known as Henliston Castle and in 1280, it was replaced by a stone building of a similar design for Edmund, Earl of Cornwall. By 1478 it had fallen into a state of disrepair. The site today is a bowling green close to the Grylls Monument, which has been in place since 1760.

Flora Day takes place annually in the town on 8 May, except when the date falls on a Sunday or Monday. Monday is Helston's market day. The Furry Dance, whose origins go by hundreds of years, is hosted by the town and attracts many visitors.

Penzance is the most westerly major town in Cornwall and is situated in the shelter of Mount's Bay.

Of the 400 prehistoric stone axes made from greenstone found all over Great Britain, petrological analysis suggests that they all come from west Cornwall. The quarry where the greenstone came from has not been located although it is thought that the Gear, a rock which lies under water approximately half a mile from Penzance, could be the site.

The earliest sign of a settlement in the area comes from the Bronze Age. Bronze Age implements that have been discovered include a palstave, a spear-head, a knife, as well as pins. Pottery and quantities of charcoal were discovered when a housing estate was built at Tredarvah, located west of Alverton.

Iron Age remains can be found at a defensive earthwork known as Lescudjack Castle. Three acres of hilltop are enclosed by a single rampart which, at one time, would have overlooked the entrance to the area from the east. Today, the area is surrounded by housing and allotments. In 2008 excavations took place to the west at Penwith College. An enclosure ditch and pottery were discovered which indicating a settlement, together with a field system with ditches and interconnecting pits which would suggest some kind of water management at one time.

At Mount Misery, to the west of Penzance, are the remains of a rampart and ditch. There is also an oval rampart and ditch at Lesingey above the St Just road. Together with the remains at Lescudjack, they overlook the coast of Penzance and Newlyn.

Previously, it was thought that there was little evidence to support a Roman occupation in Cornwall. During August 1899 two Roman coins were found in an ancient trench in Penzance Cemetery. The coins dated to the rule of Vespasian (69–79 AD). Found with the coins, which lay 8ft underground, were several cow bones, which are now kept at the Penlee House Museum. In 1934 a coin belonging to the reign of Constantine the Great was found at Alverton. It was later donated to the museum. Larger collections of coins have been found at Marazion Marsh and at Kerris in Paul parish.

The Mounts Bay Hotel and Promenade at Penzance. The earliest sign of a settlement in the area comes from the Bronze Age. Bronze implements that have been discovered include a palstave, a spear-head, a knife and pins.

Connerton was once the ancient centre of the Hundred of Penwith. Today, it lies buried beneath the beach at Gwithian Towans.

In 1284 the name 'Pensans' first appears in the Assize Roll. However, in 1750, William Borlase first mentioned the church which gave Penzance its name. He stated, 'The ancient chapel belonging to the town of Penzance may be seen in a fish cellar, near the key; it is small and as I remember had the image of the Virgin Mary in it.'

The chapel was built of local greenstone and measured about 30ft in length and 15ft wide. Some time around the year 1800, the chapel became a fish cellar. A carving of St Anthony, made of Ludgvan granite, was taken away in 1830 to be used as a wall of a pig sty. In 1850 it was further vandalised when a stranger to the area broke off parts and took them away as relics. The remains were taken to St Mary's churchyard by a mason.

In 1429, a licence for Divine Service in the Chapel of St Gabriel and St Raphael was granted, but little more is known about this chapel other than the mason referring to it as 'St Raffidy'. Adjoining the chapel is St Anthony's Gardens which contains an archway originally from the chapel site.

St Mary's dominates the skyline above Penzance harbour. St Mary's Chapel is mentioned in a document of 1548 which says that it was founded by Sir Henry Tyes, a knight and lord of the manor of Alverton. A chapel of ease, 'the chapel of Blessed Mary of Pensande' is mentioned in 1379 when Bishop Brantyngham licensed it for services.

In medieval times a market was held on a fixed day each week together with fairs on fixed dates each year. In 1332 King Edward III granted a royal charter to Alice de Lisle, sister of Lord Tyes and widow of Warin de Lisle, allowing the town to hold a market every Wednesday. A fair, lasting seven days, was held at the Feast of St Peter ad Vincula on 1 August. On 24 August, a further fair, also lasting seven days, was held at Mousehole for the feast of St Bartholomew. This fair was later moved to Penzance.

Further fairs were held in the town as it grew in importance in the fifteenth century. These took place at the Feast of the Conception of Virgin Mary (8 December), St Peter in Cathedra (22 February) and the Nativity of the Virgin Mary (8 September).

The quay at Penzance dates back before 1322 when a record shows that eight fishing boats were moored there. During 1425, 1432 and 1440, vessels in the town were licensed to carry pilgrims to the shrine of St James of Compostella in north-west Spain.

In medieval times Penzance was frequently raided by Turkish pirates. These were known as Barbary corsairs or Ottoman corsairs and were privateers who operated from North Africa.

The plague visited Penzance in the summer of 1578. Deaths increased in this year from 12 the previous year, to a total of 155. This was approximately 10 per cent of the population in the area at that time. In 1647, the plague returned again and deaths increased from 22 the previous year to 117.

Penzance and the nearby villages had been sacked many times from ships from overseas. On 23 July 1595 a Spanish fleet, including four galleys transporting 400 arquebusiers under Don Carlos de Amesquita, landed an army at Cornwall. The local militias, on seeing the men, threw down their arms and fled. However, Francis

Godolphin, the Deputy Lord Lieutenant of Cornwall and the commander of the militias along with twelve of his soldiers tried to put up a fight with little success. Amesquita's men took supplies and raided and burned Penzance and surrounding villages. Afterwards, they held a mass before leaving and successfully engaging with a fleet of forty-six Dutch ships.

In 1404 King Henry IV granted Penzance a royal market and this led to some prosperity in the town during the fifteenth, sixteenth and seventeenth centuries.

In 1512 Henry VIII granted the right to charge harbour dues and in 1614 King James I granted the town the status of a borough. The bounds of the town were defined by a charter and an artificial line was formed by a half-mile circle, taken from the market cross in the Greenmarket. When borough status was granted, it made the town independent of the County Courts. This right was held until County Councils came into being in 1888. Other privileges that came with this status included owning land and property; imposing fines for breaking bylaws; holding a civil court with jurisdiction over cases not exceeding £50 and providing a jail. The charter reconfirmed the harbour rights which were given earlier in 1512. It also granted two weekly markets which were held on Tuesdays and Thursdays. These replaced the single market which had previously been held on Wednesdays. Seven fairs were also granted. These were:

Corpus Christi, the Sunday after Whitsun;

The Thursday before St Andrew's Day (30 November);

St Peter's Day (1 August) which was first granted in 1332;

St Bartholomew's Day (24 August), which was originally granted to Mousehole but became obsolete due to the Spanish Raid of 1595;

St Mary the Virgin's Day (8 September) which was granted in 1404;

The Conception of St Mary the Virgin's Day (8 September) which was granted in 1404;

St Peter's Day in Cathedra (22 February) which was granted in 1404.

Five marks, or £3 6s 8d, was paid annually to the Crown as a perpetual rent which gave the rights granted by the charter. The rent was paid until 1832.

The arms of Penzance were originally the head of St John the Baptist on a charger and included the words 'Pensans anno Domini 1614'.

During the English Civil War Penzance was attacked by the Parliamentarian forces led by Sir Thomas Fairfax.

On 1 November 1755, as a result of the Lisbon earthquake, the sea rose at 2pm by 8ft in Penzance. It came in at great speed and fell at the same rate. The nineteenth-century French writer Arnold Boscowitz stated that a 'great loss of life and property occurred upon the coasts of Cornwall.' In 1759 a reservoir was constructed which supplied water to public pumps in the streets.

In 1801 Penzance had a population of 2,248. The population peaked in 1861 when it rose to 3,843 and thereafter declined.

In 1803 Cornwall got its first lifeboat which was bought by the people of Penzance. In 1812, however, it was sold due to lack of funds. The pier was extended in 1812 and John Matthews opened a dry dock there two years later in 1814. A branch of Nicholas Holman's foundry business was opened by the quayside and proved invaluable to the many steamships calling at the harbour.

In 1814, the Royal Geological Society of Cornwall was founded in the town and by 1817 was responsible for introducing a miner's safety tamping bar. This led to the Prince Regent becoming its patron.

In 1830 gas lighting was introduced to the town. In the same year, the Egyptian House in Chapel Street was constructed. By 1836 the old Market House was demolished and its replacement, designed by W. Harris of Bristol was completed in 1838 at Market Jew Street. The name 'Market Jew' comes from Marghas Yow which means 'Thursday Market'.

In 1836, St Mary's Church was completed and, in 1843, the Roman Catholic church was built. The building of the Promenade commenced in 1844.

When Queen Victoria came to the throne in 1837 Penzance was already an important regional centre. It became one of the first towns to petition to form a local board of health in 1848 after the Public Health Act was passed. The Board was established in 1849 and led to many facilities which enhanced public health in the town. A report by a government inspector showed that most streets were macadamised and sometimes paved. It also showed that Penzance was lit by 121 gas lamps from October to March each year. However, they were not lit when there was a full moon. Six public pumps supplied water and a further 53 private wells were in use at the time. Sewerage pipes were non-existent and waste was collected by a refuse cart.

On 11 March 1852 Penzance railway station opened with trains just running to Redruth. The line was extended to Truro on 25 August 1852 but was not linked to Plymouth until 4 May 1859. Both passengers and goods had to switch trains at Truro station as the West Cornwall line had been built using the 4ft $8\frac{1}{2}$in (1,435mm) standard gauge. However, the Cornwall Railway was built using the 7ft (2,134 mm) broad gauge. On 1 January 1866 the Great Western Railway (together with the Bristol and Exeter Railway and South Devon Railway) purchased the line and converted the line to mixed gauge using three rails so that both broad and narrow gauge trains could operate on the route. From 1 March 1867, through passenger trains ran to London. Fresh produce could now be carried to markets as far away as Bristol, London and Manchester and this greatly helped local farmers and fishermen to get the best price for their produce.

A special 'perishable' was laid on which carried potatoes, broccoli or fish. During August 1861, approximately 1,787 tons of potatoes, 867 tons of broccoli and 1,063 tons of fish were dispatched from the station. Added to this were fruit and flowers and the better climate around Penzance and on the Scilly Isles meant that they were ready for market before elsewhere and thus could fetch higher prices.

With the completion of the railway, tourism grew in the county. Visitors enjoyed the mild climate offered by Penzance and bathing machines were advertised on the beach. These had been in place since 1823 long before the advent of the railway, however. The Queen's Hotel opened on the seafront in 1861 to welcome visitors and became so successful that it was extended in 1871 and 1908.

Improvements were made to the harbour at the same time as the railway was constructed and a second pier, Albert Pier, was built on the eastern side of the harbour and completed in 1853. It provided improved shelter for shipping. In 1855 a lighthouse was built on the Old Pier.

In 1858, the Scilly Isles Steam Navigation Company was founded with the steam ship, SS *Little Western*, travelling the route. By 1870, the new West Cornwall Steam Ship Company joined the route and took over the Scilly Isles Company in 1871.

The local newspaper in 1875 compared the railway station to 'a large dog's house of the nastiest and draughtiest kind'. However, in the 1880s this area of the town was much improved. The station was rebuilt in 1880 which included the present buildings and roofed platforms.

The bottom end of Market Jew Street was made wider and a road was constructed in 1881 which linked the station to the harbour by the Ross Swing Bridge. At the same time, a sewer system was built underneath.

A larger dry dock was built to replace Matthews' original facility. In 1884, a floating harbour was put in place which included lock gates which kept the water in at low tide. In 1887 public baths were opened on the Promenade. Two years later the Morrab Gardens, complete with sub-tropical plants, was opened to the general public. In 1897, a bandstand was added to the gardens.

By 1901, the population in Penzance totalled 3,088; it declined until 1921 but grew thereafter.

An electric tramway was suggested in the 1890s which would have linked the Promenade to Newlyn and continued as a light railway to St Just. However, the proposal was dismissed.

On 31 October 1903 motor buses were introduced to the town and linked Penzance with Marazion. The buses were managed by the Great Western Railway and were introduced eleven weeks after the railway introduced a service from Helston to the Lizard. The buses proved to be hugely successful and carried 16,091 passengers in their first year. Further routes to Land's End and St Just were introduced the following year.

In August 1904 the dry dock was sold to N. Holman and Sons Limited, who had been trading in Penzance operating an engineering business since 1840. In the 1930s, new workshops were erected and the dock continued to be used by the Scilly ferries as well as various other merchant ships. Also during the 1930s, land was reclaimed alongside Albert Pier which allowed the railway station to be enlarged. The whole exercise cost £134,000 and extra platforms and sidings were added.

A new bandstand was erected on the Promenade in 1905. Six years later, in 1911, the Pavilion Theatre was opened which included a roof garden and a café.

Travelling to Penzance from other parts of the country was made much easier with the introduction of new services including the Cornish Riviera Express which left from Paddington in the morning and arrived at Penzance seven hours later.

In 1923 a new road link between the harbour and the Promenade was introduced and in 1933, St Anthony Gardens was built. The incredibly popular Jubilee Bathing Pool was built in 1935.

Many of the improvements to the town greatly attracted visitors and holidaymakers.

Marazion is situated 2 miles east of Penzance. St Michael's Mount lies half a mile offshore and, at low tide, can be walked to from the town. A boat conveys passengers back and forwards at times of high tide.

It is believed that tin smelting took place early in the town's history and the remains of an ancient bronze furnace was found nearby.

Marazion is one of the oldest chartered towns in Great Britain. Henry III granted the first charter in 1257 which was reaffirmed by Queen Elizabeth I in 1595. The earliest recorded fair was in 1070. Marazion had two major markets which were: Marghas Byghan (meaning small market) and Marghas Yow or Jew (meaning Thursday market). The name Marazion comes from a combination of the two names. Marazion was a more important town than nearby Penzance up until medieval times.

Many pilgrims visited the area and attended the Benedictine Monastery on St Michael's Mount. Amongst these was George Fox who was one of the founders of the Religious Society of Friends. He stayed in Marazion in 1656. In 1789, John Wesley, of the Wesleyan church, preached in the town.

Marazion Causeway leading to St Michael's Mount. Marazion is one of the oldest chartered towns in Great Britain. Henry III granted the first charter in 1257 which was reaffirmed by Queen Elizabeth I in 1595.

Marazion was a meeting place for men of commerce who conducted their business in the town. The main trunk road from London stopped at Marazion.

Locals made their income through fishing although the town originally didn't have a harbour. Catches at the time were landed at the harbour on St Michael's Mount. The island harbour was improved by George Blewitt in the eighteenth century and led to much prosperity.

Both tin and copper were exported from Marazion and St Michael's Mount for hundreds of years and many mines lay close by including Wheal Prosper, Wheal Crab, Wheal Rodney, Tolvadden and South Neptune. The mines were in use until the late nineteenth century when a depression hit the market. Agriculture also provided employment for many in the area. The introduction of the railway brought many tourists to the area in the late nineteenth and early twentieth centuries.

An ancient forest lies between Marazion and St Michael's Mount and at low tide or after storms, remnants of the prehistoric wood can be seen. The hazel wood was submerged in approximately 1,700BC.

People lived in the area in Neolithic times (from circa 4,000 to 2,500BC). A leaf-shaped flint arrowhead was discovered in a shallow pit on the lower eastern slope which is now part of the modern gardens. As well as the arrowhead, pieces of flint have been found and it is thought that they at least date from the Mesolithic period (circa 8,000 to 3500BC). At this time, Britain was still joined to mainland Europe via Doggerland.

During this time, the mount would have been dry ground surrounded by a marshy forest. A collection of copper weapons were found on nearby Marazion Marsh. It is suggested that defensive stony banks on the north-eastern slopes date to the early first millennium BC and are possibly part of a cliff castle. The mount may have been the location for 'the island of Ictis', which was described as a tin trading centre by Diodorus Siculus, a Sicilian-Greek historian, writing in the first century BC. It is believed that the mount was the site of a monastery in the eighth to early eleventh centuries. It was given to the Norman Abbey of Mont Saint-Michel by Edward the Confessor. After the war in France it was given to the Abbess and Convent of Syon at Isleworth, Middlesex in 1424 when its association ended with Mont Saint-Michel and any connection with Looe Island (dedicated to the Archangel Michael).

During the twelfth century the monastic buildings were constructed. An earthquake in 1275 destroyed the original Priory Church but this was rebuilt in the late fourteenh century.

In 1193, during the reign of King Richard I, the mount was captured by Sir Henry de la Pomeroy, on behalf of Prince John. In 1473, John de Vere, the 13th Earl of Oxford, seized and held the mount against 6,000 of Edward IV's men. The siege lasted twenty-three weeks.

The mount was occupied by Perkin Warbeck in 1497. Sir Humphrey Arundell, the Governor of St Michael's Mount, led a rebellion during 1549. In the reign of Queen Elizabeth I, it was given to Robert Cecil, Earl of Salisbury. His son later sold to Sir Francis Bassett. During the English Civil War, Sir Arthur Bassett, the brother of Sir Francis, held the mount against the Parliamentary forces until July 1646.

The castle and chapel on St Michael's Mount have belonged to the St Aubyn family since about 1650 although the earliest buildings on the island date back to the twelfth century.

St Michael's Mount and Marazion were also greatly affected by the after effects of the Lisbon earthquake of 1755.

Little is recorded of the village before the beginning of the 1700s, apart from that there were several fishermen's cottages as well as a few monastic dwellings. After improvements to the harbour in 1727, St Michael's Mount became a prosperous seaport. By 1811 there were fifty-three houses and four streets on the island. In 1821, the pier was extended and the population grew taking the number of inhabitants to 221. Also on the island at the time were three schools and a Wesleyan chapel. The three public houses were mainly used by visiting sailors.

After major improvements to the harbour at Penzance and the railway was extended in 1852, the village at St Michael's Mount declined and some houses were demolished. During the Victorian period there was an underground, funicular narrow gauge railway constructed, but this was short-lived. The funicular took visitors' luggage up to the house and at first was seen as a great labour-saving device. Thought to be Britain's last functionally operational 4ft 6in railway, it is still there today but remains unused.

Towards the end of the nineteenth century, the remains of an anchorite were found within a tomb inside the Mount's domestic chapel.

The year before the war, Neville Chamberlain travelled to Germany to appease Hitler. Pictured beside him is the German Foreign Minister Joachim von Ribbentrop. Hitler promised Ribbentrop St Michael's Mount should Germany win the war.

The Keigwin Arms at Mousehole. In 1595, Mousehole was destroyed in a raid on Mount Bay by the Spaniard, Carlos de Amésquita. The only remaining building from that time is the Keigwin Arms, the local inn.

During the Second World War, the mount was fortified due to the fear of a German invasion in the years 1940 to 1941. Three pillboxes remain on the island.

Joachim von Ribbentrop, the former Nazi foreign minister and one time ambassador to London, intended to live on the mount should Germany win the war. Before the war General von Ribbentrop had frequently visited Cornwall.

Mousehole is approximately 2½ miles south of Penzance and lies on the shore of Mount's Bay. Until the sixteenth century, Mousehole (along with Marazion) was one of the main ports of Mount's Bay. At one time, the village had several fairs and markets. This included the charter for a market on Tuesdays and a fair for three days at the festival of St Barnabas. The charter was granted to Henry de Tyes in 1292.

Mousehole came within the authority of the Manor of Alverton and all early charters for markets and fairs were associated with this manorial estate.

In 1595 Mousehole was destroyed in a raid on Mount's Bay by the Spaniard, Carlos de Amésquita. The only remaining building from that time is the Keigwin Arms, the local inn. There is a plaque outside the inn which reads, 'Squire Jenkyn Keigwin was killed here 23 July 1595 defending this house against the Spaniards'.

The village was once well-known for its historic harbourside hotel, The Lobster Pot. In the 1930s it was a guest house which was run by Wyn Henderson, a friend of the poet Dylan Thomas. Today it has been replaced by luxury apartments. It was in the Lobster Pot in 1938 that Dylan Thomas spent his honeymoon after marrying Caitlin Macnamara at the Penzance registry office.

Many festivals are still held at Mousehole. On every 19 December since the lifeboat disaster of 1981, the lights have been turned off in the village in memory of the victims. Tom Bawcock's Eve, held on 23 December each year, celebrates that local resident Tom Bawcock ended a famine in the sixteenth century by fishing in stormy weather. This festival

The harbour at Mousehole as it is today. The village was once well-known for its historic harbourside hotel, The Lobster Pot. In the 1930s, it was a guest house which was run by Wyn Henderson, a friend of the poet Dylan Thomas.

Porth Chapel Beach, Porthcurno. The village name comes from the sixteenh century Cornish spelling 'Porth Cornowe' which means a 'cove or landing place of horns or pinnacles'.

inspired the book *The Mousehole Cat*, written by Antonia Barber. From this festival, 'Star Gazey Pie' originated. It consists of a mixed fish, egg and potato pie with fish heads protruding through the pastry. Every other year, the village also holds a small maritime festival which is called 'Sea, Salt and Sail'.

The small village of **Porthcurno** lies 6½ miles west of Penzance and 2½ miles away from Land's End. The village's name comes from the sixteenth century Cornish spelling 'Porth Cornowe' which means a 'cove or landing place of horns or pinnacles'.

Porthcurno is well-known for its important international submarine communications cable station. In the late nineteenth century, the small beach at Porthcurno became famous worldwide as the British termination of early submarine telegraph cables. The first of these was landed in 1870 and was part of an international link which stretched from Great Britain to India. The beach at Porthcurno was chosen instead of the busy port of Falmouth because it was felt that there was a reduced risk of damage to the cables caused by ships' anchors.

The Eastern Telegraph Company (ETC) Limited was founded in 1872 and took over the operation of cables. They went on to build a cable office in Porthcurno Valley. In 1928, they merged with Marconi's Wireless Telegraph Company Limited and formed Imperial and International Communications Limited. In 1934, this became Cable and Wireless Limited.

Between the two wars, the cable office at Porthcurno operated fourteen cables and for a while, became the largest submarine cable station in the world. During the Second World War Porthcurno was thought to be a vulnerable point for an enemy invasion and thus was heavily defended and fortified. A small guard of special constables was placed on duty at the cable office and house at the beginning of the war and later a squadron of soldiers was posted there and camped on the former bowling green.

The valley at Porthcurno was declared a protected place and over 300 men were deployed to the area to guard the station.

Residents and visitors in Porthcurno were issued with passes which had to be shown when requested. Many mock attacks were staged in the village. Amongst the defences were several pillboxes and a petroleum warfare beach flame barrage.

Approximately 867 bombs fell on the Penzance area and 3,957 houses were damaged or destroyed. However, the communications equipment at Porthcurno only suffered slight damage to an antenna when a bomb fell nearby at Rospletha Farm, located at the top of the hill about half a mile to the west of the cable office.

The nearby Minack Theatre was built by Rowena Cade during the 1930s. Its dramatic open-air setting with the backdrop of the sea has made it popular with theatre goers for over seventy years.

Sennen lies 8 miles south-west of Penzance and is the first village in Cornwall, if travelling from Land's End. Several of the

The Minack Theatre at Porthcurno. The theatre was built by Rowena Cade during the 1930s. Its dramatic open-air setting with the backdrop of the sea has made it popular with theatre goers for over 70 years.

Sennen Cove and the Lifeboat slip. Sennen lies 8 miles south-west of Penzance. It is the first village in Cornwall, if travelling from Land's End.

submarine telecommunications cables previously mentioned land at Sennen Cove. From here, they are connected by landlines to the cable equipment at Skewjack.

Sennen Cove was once a busy fishing village and the trade continues today but now much of its income comes from tourism. In 1908, a breakwater was built which protects the small group of fishing vessels.

Sennen Cove was once a major seine fishery in Cornwall. In Edwardian times, as many as 12,000 could be netted in a single catch.

St Just lies on the B3306 which connects St Ives to the A30. Prehistoric remains lie close by to the town, including Ballowall

Fishermen mending crab pots at Sennen Cove. Sennen Cove was once a major seine fishery in Cornwall. In Edwardian times, as many as 12,000 could be caught in a single catch.

The Square at St Just in the 1950s. St Just is one of the oldest mining districts in the county and there are remains of ancient pre-industrial mines as well as more recent mining activity.

Barrow, a chambered tomb. St Just is one of the oldest mining districts in the county and there are remains of ancient pre-industrial mines as well as more recent mining activity.

The parish church of St Just was rebuilt in 1336 and dedicated by John Grandisson, the Bishop of Exeter. Only the chancel remains from this time and most of the church dates to the fifteenth century. There are also two Methodist chapels.

Seven Cornish crosses can be found in the parish. Two are located in the vicarage garden and one is built into the church wall. The other crosses are at Leswidden, Nanquidno and Kenidjack.

St Ives, which once relied for its living on the fishing trade, is extremely popular with tourists today and there are many second homes there. Artists travel to the area because of the quality of light and the Tate St Ives gallery is located there.

Local legend tells of the arrival of the Irish saint Ia of Cornwall during the fifth century. The parish church is named after her and the name St Ives is derived from this.

The busy beach at Carbis Bay in St Ives in the 1950s. Local legend tells of the arrival of the Irish saint Ia of Cornwall during the fifth century. The parish church is named after her and the name St Ives is derived from this.

The Sloop Inn dates from 1312 and has been popular with fishermen for hundreds of years. It is one of the oldest inns in Cornwall.

During the Prayer Book Rebellion of 1549 the English provost marshal, Anthony Kingston, visited St Ives. He invited the Portreeve (port marshal), John Payne, to lunch at the Sloop Inn. While they were eating, Kingston requested that Payne erect the gallows. On leaving the inn, the Portreeve and the Provost Marshal strolled down to the gallows. Once there, the Provost Marshal ordered the Portreeve to mount the gallows and he was hanged for being a 'busy rebel'.

In 1597 two Spanish ships from the Spanish Harbour moored at St Ives while seeking shelter from a storm. They were captured by Sir Walter Raleigh and his warship, *Warspite*. The prisoners gave vital information regarding the Armada's objectives.

St Ives was once the most important fishing port on the north coast of Cornwall. The trade dates back to medieval times and before. Between 1776 and 1770, John Smeaton built the town's pier which was later lengthened.

Seagulls enjoying the fishermen's catch at St Ives. St Ives was once the most important fishing port on the north coast of Cornwall. The trade dates back to medieval times and before.

From 1747 to 1756 the amount of pilchards sent from the four major ports of Falmouth, Fowey, Penzance and St Ives was annually 30,000 hogsheads. This made a total of 900 million fish. Even larger catches were made in 1790 and 1796. In 1847 the total export of pilchards from the county amounted to 40,883 hogsheads or 122 million fish. The main part of the catch was sent to Italy. In 1830, 6,400 hogsheads were dispatched to Mediterranean ports.

St Ives has had its own lifeboat since 1840. The Royal National Lifeboat Institution constructed a boathouse at Porthgwidden beach in 1867. It was difficult to launch the boat from this location so, soon after, the building was relocated to Fore Street. In 1911 a new boathouse was erected on the quay. In 1939, seven crewmen were killed during the early hours of 23 January. At the time, there was a Force 10 storm, blowing gusts of up to 100 miles per hour. A ship reported in trouble off Cape Cornwall and at 3 o'clock, the lifeboat, *John and Sara Eliza Stych*, was launched. It met the full force of the storm and capsized three times. With its propeller fouled, it drifted across St Ives Bay. Four men were lost when it first capsized and

Fishermen mending their nets on Smeaton's Pier, St Ives in the 1940s. The pier was built between 1767 and 1770. It was later lengthened.

another man was lost the second time. The third capsize left only one man on board. He made it ashore before the boat was wrecked on rocks at Godrevy Point.

The railway arrived in 1877 and greatly boosted the tourism trade. Victorian holidaymakers were drawn to the Cornish coast and much of the town was developed in the late nineteenth century.

CHAPTER 7

Hayle to Padstow

Hayle is a small town situated at the mouth of the Hayle River. It lies approximately 7 miles north-east of Penzance. The area has been inhabited since at least the Bronze Age although Hayle, as it is today, was built mainly during the industrial revolution of the eighteenth century.

Above Carnsew Pool, there is evidence of an Iron Age settlement, at the fort on the hill, today the location of the Plantation.

Hayle played a major part during the Neolithic tin industry, trading with the Irish and Breton people as well as with the Phoenicians of the eastern Mediterranean. Remnants of imported pottery have been found in the area, including Romano/Grecian Amphorae.

Romans occupied the area at one point and coins from this time have been discovered as recently as 2017. It is thought that the Romans had a presence around the Hayle estuary and many believe that the rectangular churchyard at St Uny's Church at Lelant, which lies on the western shore of the estuary, was built within the footprint of a long since disappeared Roman fort. At the time, the estuary would have been a lot deeper and vessels could travel as far as where the present St Erth Bridge is located. At one time, the tide flowed in and out of what is now Foundry Square in the town.

When the Romans left the area, Christian missionaries arrived, many from Ireland. Saint Samson and Saint Petroc are both said to have landed in Cornwall at the Hayle Estuary during the fifth century.

The area was held by the Breton exile, Tewdwr Mawr, in the sixth century. Several inscribed stones date from this time two of which can be found at Phillack. Another stone, the most noteworthy one, was

A 1950s view of the beach at Hayle Towans. Hayle played a major part during the neolithic tin industry trading with the Irish and Breton people, as well as trading with the Phoenicians of the eastern Mediterranean.

discovered during the building of a road in the grounds of Carnsew. This is today set into a bank at the Plantation, a public park. Workmen found the stone in December 1843. It was in a horizontal position, buried 4ft down but unfortunately when it was removed, it broke into three parts. It was fixed into a nearby wall by a local resident and remains there, together with a replica. An inscription in Latin appears on the stone but today, this is unreadable. On the replica, the translation of the Latin phrase reads, 'Here Cenui fell asleep who was born in 500. Here in his tomb he lies, he lived 33 years.'

Hayle as a port continued to prove important throughout the Middle Ages and the town grew greatly during the Industrial Revolution.

Hayle did not exist in the time of the Domesday survey in 1086 although a number of nearby farmsteads are recorded. Evidence of settlements around the Hayle Estuary did not appear until 1130. At that time Phillack Church and the surrounding buildings were recorded as 'Egloshayle', which translates to the church (eglos) on the estuary (heyl). The church was dedicated originally to St Felec and this is where the name Phillack comes from.

Hayle is first properly recorded in 1265 but then only consisted of a few dwellings and several scattered farms.

During the Industrial Revolution, Hayle originally imported coal and exported ore from its port. It was dwarfed by nearby Angarrack, where in 1704 a tin smelter was built. Hayle proved to be a handy port to land coal from South Wales which was then transported to Angarrack by mule. During 1710 a copper and tin smelter was built at Mellanear Farm beside the Mellanear stream and this prospered for many years thereafter.

In the 1740s the first major development at Hayle was the building of a modern quay by John Curnow. This proved beneficial to the growing mining industry. In 1758 a copper smelter was set up at Ventonleague by the Cornish Copper Company which had moved from Camborne. This was hugely successful and a canal was constructed to allow vessels to travel right up to the smelter. Land on both sides of the creek was purchased for industrial use and to house workers.

Large amounts of waste were produced by the smelting process. The copper slag was used as building material. The slag was turned into large bricks and cost 9d for 20 but were given free to the workers of the Cornish Copper Company so that they could build their own houses. Both Sea Lane and Black Road were constructed using these bricks.

Waste was also used to fill in the upper part of Copperhouse Creek which created Wilson's Pool and separated it from Copperhouse Pool. The Pool was afterwards used as a tidal reservoir which let vessels travel up to the dock, approximately where the Co-op was once situated. They were used to flush or sluice the channel to make sure that it was kept clear of sand and silt.

During 1779 a local blacksmith from Carnhell Green named John Harvey built a small foundry and engineering works in Hayle. This is now known as Foundry. At the time it supplied the local mining industry. The foundry prospered and by 1800 more than fifty people were employed there. It continued to thrive and was linked to several important engineers and entrepreneurs including Richard Trevithick, William West and Arthur Woolf.

Harvey and Co are well-known for making beam engines which are considered some of the finest ever constructed. These were used in Cornish mines and dispatched worldwide. They also manufactured hand tools as well as ocean-going ships, including the SS *Cornubia* and the world's first steam-powered rock-boring machine.

As Hayle prospered, the owners of the foundry and smelter owners invested in the local mining industry.

Between 1831 until 1861 the Hayle and Bristol Steam Packet Company operated Steam Packet services. From 1837 it connected with the recently opened Hayle to Redruth Railway. Originally the terminus for the railway was at Foundry Square. It was designed to carry both passengers and goods. In 1843 steam was introduced to the Hayle section of the line but, at the time, only light engines could be used due to the construction of the railway. During 1852 a new line opened which stretched over the valley along the Angarrack viaduct. It passed through Hayle on wooden supports over Foundry Square. These were later replaced with the present stone pillars. The Harbour branch line remained open until 1982 when the station buildings and signal box were removed at the same time. The original station in Foundry Square was demolished just after the Second World War.

Harvey's of Hayle achieved prosperity until the mid-nineteenth century but, like other foundries and engineering works in Hayle, slowly declined. In 1903 the engineering works and Foundry closed.

In 1866 a lifeboat was stationed at Hayle. A boathouse was built for the lifeboat in 1897 but it was eventually closed in 1920.

In 1888 the National Explosive works set up at Upton Towans. It was known at 'Dynamite Towans' by the locals. Originally, the company supplied the mining trade but went on to supply the military. During the First World War, it employed over 1,500 people. In 1920 the manufacture of explosives ceased although explosives were still stored at the site until the 1960s.

In 1910, the Hayle Power Station was opened on Harvey's Towans. It was originally coal-fired with the coal being shipped from South Wales. The station remained open until 1977.

Between the two World Wars several small works were established on North Quay. These included a glass works, a small oil depot and an ICI plant which produced bromine. The additive increased the power of aircraft including Hurricanes, Spitfires, Lancasters and Mosquitoes.

The town of **Camborne** is 3 miles to the west of Redruth. The first mention of Camborne was in 1181. However, the ruins of a Romano-British villa were found at Magor Farm, Illogan, near Camborne in 1931 suggesting that its history stretches much further back. There are several early Christian sites including an inscribed altar stone which, today, is in the Church of St Martin and St Meriadoc. The sites date to the tenth century.

Mining was first recorded in the area in the 1400s which involved early exploitation of the small streams by cutting through the mineralised area and from shallow mines. Adit mining was first recorded in the sixteenth century.

A busy Edwardian scene in Commercial Square, Camborne. A tram waits for passengers in the background. The Commercial Hotel can be seen on the right.

By 1708, Camborne had a charter to hold markets as well as three fairs a year.

The first chapel was built in 1806 and the population grew to 4,377 in 1841. The town gas works opened in 1834.

Camborne was the centre for the Cornish tin and copper mining industry, especially during the later eighteenth and early nineteenth centuries. The area was transformed by the mining boom and Camborne and the Redruth district became the richest mining areas in the world.

On Christmas Eve 1801, the Puffing Devil, which was a steam-powered road locomotive built by Camborne engineer Richard Trevithick, travelled up Camborne Hill. It was the world's first self-propelled passenger carrying vehicle. Trevithick, the son of a miner, was born in Penponds in 1771. He was later educated at Camborne School.

The town of **Redruth** is located 9 miles west of Truro. The town originally fell within the Penwith Hundred but developed away from the original settlement, which was close to where the present day Churchtown district of Redruth stands today.

Early settlers exploiting the tin, lead and copper in the area stayed by a crossing in the river where they began extracting metal ores. This work turned the colour of the river red.

Redruth was originally a small market town which was overshadowed by its neighbours. When there was a demand for copper ore in the eighteenth century, its prosperity grew. Copper ore had generally been discarded by the Cornish tin-mining industry, however, it was now required to make brass, which was an essential metal used during the Industrial Revolution. Rich in copper ore deposits, Redruth grew to become one of the largest and most prosperous mining areas in Britain.

During the 1880s and 1890s, Redruth gained a number of institutions including a School of Mines and Art School in 1882–83, St Andrew's Church in 1883 and the Free Library in 1895. In 1880 the Mining Exchange was built and was used for the trading of mineral stock. Victoria Park was laid out in the late 1800s and commemorated the Golden Jubilee of Queen Victoria.

An earlier busy scene showing Fore Street in Redruth. In 1880, the Mining Exchange was built in the town and was used for the trading of mineral stock.

Fore Street, Redruth in the 1940s. Rich in copper ore deposits, Redruth grew to become one of the largest and most prosperous mining areas in Britain during the eighteenth and nineteenth centuries.

The Cornish mining industry declined at the end of the nineteenth century and most of Britain's copper ore was imported from elsewhere. Many miners left the area and emigrated to find work mining in the Americas, Australasia and South Africa.

Porthtowan is a small village on the north Atlantic coast approximately 2½ miles north of Redruth. The village has a long mining history and one of its most prominent buildings is a former engine house which has now been converted for residential use. Allen's Corn Mill operated in the village between 1752 and 1816.

The area became popular with holidaymakers during Victorian and Edwardian times and is still popular today with tourists and attracts many surfers.

St Agnes lies 5 miles north of Redruth and is a popular coastal tourist spot. Several ancient archaeological sites are located in the area.

An early view of Porthtowan showing a tin mine on the horizon. The village has a long mining history and one of its most prominent buildings is a former engine house which has now been converted for residential use.

Mesolithic fragments, dating from 10,000 to 4,000BC were found at New Downs and West Polberro.

Bronze Age barrows exist in the area. At the time, St Agnes would have been rich in both copper and tin, essential for making bronze. In the Iron Age a hillfort was built at Caer Dane, south-east of Perranporth. At one time, it had three concentric defensive walls which surrounded an inner, topmost ring. The enclosed round of St Piran's was approximately 660ft wide and possibly was a performance area. During the Middle Ages it was converted to a theatre and today is still sometimes used for this purpose.

Other prehistoric geographic features include the Bolster Bank at Porth, which is an univallate earthen boundary about 2 miles long. It is probable that it was used for defensive purposes and would have protected the heath as well as the tin resources. On the land side of St Agnes Beacon, evidence of the bulwark can be sighted sporadically all the way from Bolster Farm to Goonvrea Farm and towards Wheal Freedom and then onto Chapel Coombes. Much of the boundary today has been levelled but it is at its highest by Bolster Farm and Goonvrea where it is about 11ft high.

Between 410 and 1,066AD the first chapel was built in St Agnes. It is thought to have been built as an early Celtic church. At that time it would have had an enclosure. Around 1482 the Church of St Agnes was constructed on the same location. At Chapel Porth there once stood a medieval chapel. There was also a holy well and a post medieval storehouse on the site. In 1780 the chapel was destroyed but the holy well remained until 1820.

A tin working site existed at St Agnes during the Middle Ages as well as tin works at Wheal Coates, near the Chapel Porth area cliffs. Also during the Middle Ages, a manor was built in St Agnes. Between 1700 and 1800 a house was constructed at the location of the previous manor. Today, it is a convalescent home. A Trevellas country house was also built during this period.

A chapel was built sometime between 1540 and the 1800s and was located north of Mawla. Later on the building was used as a shed

Churchtown, St Agnes in the 1940s. Several ancient archaeological sites are located in the area. Mesolithic fragments, dating from 10,000 to 4,000BC were found at New Downs and West Polberro.

for cows. By 1847 it was little more than a ruin. The St John the Baptist church in Mount Hawke got its font from this church.

The Miners Arms Public House was built in Mithian and dates from the 1600s. Modern mining methods were employed in the 1800s with Wheal Lushington being the biggest tin mining operation in the area at the time. It was operational by 1808 and smelting was also performed at Wheal Lushington. Modern mining procedures were used at Blue Hills Mine from about 1810 until 1897. Previously, there had been former mining activities in that area from before 1780. Several copper, tin and arsenic mines were in use during the eighteenth, nineteenth and some well into the twentieth century.

There was a railway station on the Perranporth line from 1903 until 1963. This was used for the mining industry.

During the Second World War, Cameron Camp, which was also known as the 10th Light Anti-Aircraft Practice Camp, Royal Artillery, was constructed on the site of a Napoleonic Wars target. The camp was named after a local landowner and served as an army camp, slit trench and anti-aircraft battery. After the war the camp housed local residents. It was flattened in 1971.

The beach at Perranporth during the early 1960s. On 7 March 1901 the Voorspoed *ran aground during a northerly gale in Perran Bay. It had been on its way from Cardiff to Bahia. The wreck was one of the last to be looted in the region.*

Perranporth is a small seaside town 6 miles south-west of Newquay. It is popular with tourists and surfers.

On 7 March 1901, the *Voorspoed*, on its way from Cardiff to Bahia, ran aground during a northerly gale in Perran Bay. The wreck was one of the last to be looted in the region.

In the Second World War, Perranporth Airfield was constructed and used as an RAF fighter station. Today it is a civil airfield.

Perranporth was connected to the railway up until the 1960s. It was part of the Truro and Newquay Railway which ran from Chacewater to Newquay. The principal intermediate stop was Perranporth station. Perranporth also had a second station, known as Perranporth Beach Halt.

Newquay is a popular seaside resort and fishing port 12 miles north of Truro. Several prehistoric burial mounds exist in the area. There were once as many as fifteen barrows, but today only a few still exist. Excavations in the past have revealed charred cooking pots and a coarse pottery burial urn which contained the remains of a Bronze Age chieftain, buried approximately 3,500 years ago.

At Trethellan Farm, evidence was found of a Bronze Age village in 1987. Signs of a settlement in the area include an Iron Age fort from where local iron resources were exploited. The site is said to have been occupied from the third century BC to the fifth century AD.

The inlet where Newquay Harbour stands today gave a natural protection from poor weather and because of this, a small fishing village grew up around the area. The village isn't mentioned in the Domesday Book but a nearby house, today known as 'Treninnick Tavern', is recorded.

In the fifteenth century the village was known as 'Towan Blystra'. The area was exposed to winds from the north east so, in 1439, the local burgess applied to the Bishop of Exeter for money to build a new quay, which is where the town's current name comes from.

The census of 1801 noted that there were approximately 1,300 people living in the area. In 1832, work began on building the new harbour. In 1882 Newquay parish was created.

Tourism began to grow in 1876 with the arrival of passenger trains to the area. Several hotels were built at the beginning of the

Porth Bridge at Newquay. Several prehistoric burial mounds exist in the area. There were once as many as fifteen barrows, but today only a few still exist.

Tolcarne Beach at Newquay. In the fifteenth century, the village was known as 'Towan Blystra'.

A 1920s photo showing Towan Beach at Newquay. Tourism began to grow in 1876 with the arrival of passenger trains to the area. Several hotels were built at the beginning of the nineteenth century to accommodate visitors.

nineteenth century to accommodate visitors. These included the Victoria in East Street, the Atlantic and the Headland. Three new churches were constructed soon after 1901.

The town grew eastwards and stretched towards the railway station. In 1930, Station Road became Cliff Road. The houses at Narrowcliff were converted into hotels. Narrowcliff was originally known as Narrowcliff Promenade before it became Narrowcliff Road.

The town grew steadily with new houses and hotels built. Until the early twentieth century, Newquay was well-known for its pilchards and a Huer's Hut stands above the harbour. Newquay's current crest includes four pilchards and its motto is 'Ro An Mor', which is Cornish for 'from the sea'.

The town of **Bodmin** lies south-west of Bodmin Moor.

In the sixth century, St Petroc established a monastery in Bodmin and the town was given the alternate name of Petrockstow. During the Norman conquest, the monastery had some of its lands taken away. However, by the time of the Domesday Book, it still had eighteen manors which included Bodmin, Padstow and Rialton.

A 1940s scene showing Fore Street in Bodmin. In the sixth century, St Petroc established a monastery in Bodmin and the town was given the alternate name of Petrockstow.

The town is one of the oldest in the county and the only large Cornish settlement noted in the Domesday Book.

During the fifteenth century, the Norman church of St Petroc was greatly rebuilt and today is one of the largest churches in the county.

Bodmin prospered because of its local tin industry.

The town's name comes from the Cornish 'Bod-meneghy', which means 'dwelling of or by the sanctuary of monks'. Over the years, various spellings have been recorded including Botmenei in 1100, Bodmen in 1253, Bodman in 1377 and Bodmyn in 1522.

A stone built into a wall of a summer house in Lancarffe suggests a settlement in the area during the Middle Ages. It is believed to date from between the sixth and eighth centuries.

There was once three Cornish crosses at Bodmin and these were recorded by Arthur Langdon in 1896. One stood near the Berry Tower, one was outside Bodmin Gaol and the other was in a field near Castle Street Hill. A further cross, Carminow Cross, stands at a road junction just south-east of the town.

During the mid fourteenth century, half of the population of Bodmin were killed by the Black Death. This amounted to approximately 1,500 people.

The town became the centre for several Cornish uprisings. In 1497 the Cornish Rebellion, was led by Michael An Gof, a blacksmith from St Keverne and Thomas Flamank, a lawyer from Bodmin. Together with an army, they marched to Blackheath in London before they were defeated by 10,000 men of the King's army commanded by Baron Daubeny. In the autumn of 1497, the Pretender Perkin Warbeck tried to take the throne from Henry VII. Warbeck was hailed as King Richard IV in Bodmin but Henry soon put down the uprising.

During 1549 Cornishmen, together with rebels in neighbouring Devon, rose up when the Protestant king, Edward VI, tried to impose a new Prayer Book. Many in the two counties were still staunch Catholics. A Cornish army was raised in Bodmin and marched across the border to attack Exeter. The conflict was known as the Prayer Book Rebellion. A total of 4,000 people were killed during the fighting.

Fore Street in Bodmin during the 1950s. The town is one of the oldest in the county and the only large Cornish settlement noted in the Domesday Book.

Wadebridge lies on the River Camel, 5 miles upstream from Padstow. The settlement was originally known as 'Wade' before the bridge was built. An early crossing included a chapel on each side of the river. Kings chapel stood on the north side and St Michael's on the south side. People prayed for a safe passage at the chapels before they crossed at low tide, giving thanks to God in the other chapel once they were safely across.

In 1312 a charter was granted for a market at Wade. A ferry operated for a time. However, the Reverend Thomas Lovibond became dismayed at the amount of people and animals who lost their lives while crossing the River Camel. He suggested building a bridge and this was completed in 1468. Wade afterwards became known as Wadebridge. A toll was charged to cross the bridge when it was first completed.

In 1646, during the English Civil War, Oliver Cromwell led 500 dragoons and 1,000 horsemen towards Bodmin to seize the bridge as it lay in a strategic position.

The bridge was widened in 1853 from almost 10ft to 16½ft. In 1952 it was further widened and again in 1963, making it 39ft.

In 1897 typhoid broke out in the area caused by contaminated drinking water. This led to Wadebridge taking decisive action to install proper water supplies and a more efficient disposal of sewage.

The Bodmin and Wadebridge Railway stretched from Wadebridge to Wenfordbridge and had branch lines to Bodmin and Ruthernbridge. It was built at a cost of £35,000. The plan was for the line to carry sand from the Camel Estuary to inland farms to be used for fertiliser. The line was opened on 30 September 1834 and the locomotive, Camel, steamed to Wadebridge with a train load of 400 passengers. A second locomotive was ordered. The makers, thinking that the first train had been called after an animal and not the river, named the second locomotive, 'Elephant'. The last train left in 1967 before cutbacks were introduced and the line closed. The line has since become the Camel Trail used by walkers and cyclists.

Molesworth Street in Wadebridge in the 1950s. The settlement was originally known as 'Wade' before the bridge was built.

A later shot showing Molesworth Street in Wadebridge in the 1960s. The Reverend Thomas Lovibond became dismayed at the amount of people and animals who lost their lives while crossing the River Camel. He suggested building a bridge and this was completed in 1468. Wade afterwards became known as Wadebridge.

Wadebridge provided the main trade route on the river before the railway arrived. Coasters brought goods from Bristol and coal from South Wales. Timber was brought from the Baltic and stone from inland was sent to various destinations throughout England. The railway originally linked with the river traffic, being designed to distribute sand via the river to the local farms. The sand was brought from Padstow on barges and had formerly been taken as far as Michaelstow and Blisland.

By 1880 quays were located on both sides of the river beneath the bridge, the quay on the west bank being served by the railway. A sand dock was built further upstream from the bridge at the point where the Treguddick Brook meets the River Camel. In 1895, however, this was filled in.

In the 1900s ships brought cargos of fertiliser as well as grain and coal. Flour was also delivered from Ranks at Avonmouth. By the 1950s the river had silted up so much that the ketch *Agnes* was the final vessel to deliver a cargo to Wadebridge in 1955.

When cracks appeared in the rock on which the Eddystone Lighthouse was standing, James Nicholas Douglass was commissioned to build a new lighthouse in 1877. Granite came from De Lank quarry and was brought to Wadebridge where stonemasons carefully dovetailed each piece of stone. As each layer was finished and checked to make sure it fitted the layer above, it was dispatched to the Eddystone rocks by sea. In 1882 the lighthouse was completed. The road where the masons tolled was eventually renamed Eddystone Road.

The town of **Padstow** lies 5 miles north-west of Wadebridge. It was originally called Petroc-stow, Petroc-stowe, or 'Petrock's Place', named after the Welsh missionary, St Petroc, who landed at Trebetherick in about 500AD. In 981AD, 'Petroces stow' was raided by Vikings. A monastery existed in the area up until this point but the monks fled inland to Bodmin taking with them relics of St Petroc.

Padstow is noted in the Domesday Book of 1086. The record shows that it was held by Bodmin Monastery. Land existed for four

A 1930s view of the harbour at Padstow. The town was originally called Petroc-stow, Petroc-stowe, or 'Petrock's Place', named after the Welsh missionary, St Petroc, who landed at Trebetherick in about 500AD.

ploughs, five villeins who had two ploughs, six smallholders and 24 acres of pasture. Its value was estimated at 10s.

During the medieval period, Padstow was known as Aldestowe which translated to 'old place'. Today, the area attracts many tourists and, because of its association with TV chef Rick Stein, is commonly called 'Padstein'.

CHAPTER 8

Rock to Bude

Rock lies opposite Padstow and is a coastal fishing village popular with holidaymakers. Rock Dunes have been designated as a Site of Special Scientific Interest for their flora and geology.

In 1303 the original name for Rock was Penmayn which is Cornish for 'the end' or 'head of stones'. It was also called Blaketorre, Black Tor in 1337. By the eighteenth century this became Black Rock and was eventually shortened to Rock.

Rock is well-known for its well-established centre for water sports which include dinghy racing, waterskiing, windsurfing, and sailing. The headquarters of the Rock Sailing Club is located in a converted warehouse and is now a local landmark. Rock has the county's highest proportion of second homes.

The Black Tor Ferry runs between Rock and Padstow. The area has been called 'Britain's Saint-Tropez' and the 'Kensington of Cornwall' due to its popularity with well-off holidaymakers.

Polzeath, 6 miles north-west of Wadebridge, is in the parish of St Minver and today is popular with surfers and other water sport enthusiasts.

In 1590 Shilla Mill, at the edge of Polzeath, was built but it ceased working as a mill in 1885. In 1911 a Methodist chapel was erected at Chapel Corner on the road towards Trebetherick.

Until 1934 the main street in the village crossed the stream by ford. A footbridge was originally provided for pedestrians but this was sometimes destroyed by winter storms. In 1934 a permanent road bridge was constructed.

The village street at Polzeath. In 1590 Shilla Mill, at the edge of Polzeath, was built but it ceased working as a mill in 1885.

Port Isaac is a small and picturesque fishing village which, today, is used in the filming of the popular TV series, *Doc Martin*. The closest towns are Wadebridge and Camelford.

The pier at Port Isaac was built in the time of Henry VIII. Many of the buildings in the village date to the eighteenth and nineteenth centuries. Then its prosperity relied on local coastal freight and fishing. The port took delivery of cargoes of coal, wood, stone, ores, limestone, salt, pottery and heavy goods which were carried away along its narrow streets.

Before the sixteenth century, pilchard fishing took place in the area. By 1850 there were forty-nine fishing boats together with four fish cellars and fishing is still a source of income today. There are ninety listed buildings in the village all of which are Grade II.

In 1869 the Port Isaac lifeboat station was set up after the delivery of two lifeboats, *Richard* and *Sarah*.

The town of **Camelford** is 10 miles north of Bodmin. In the past the town has been linked to the legendary Camelot, as well as to the Battle of Camlann. Camelford has also been linked to Gafulford, where a battle against the West Saxons took place. However, it has been suggested that this is more likely to have taken place at Galford

Fore Street at Port Isaac in the 1930s. The pier at Port Isaac was built in the time of Henry VIII. Many of the buildings in the village date to the eighteenh and nineteenth centuries.

in Devon. Slaughterbridge was also supposed to be the location of a battle. However, the word 'slaughter' has been misinterpreted and actually means 'marsh' in Anglo-Saxon.

The village of **Tintagel** is linked with legends surrounding King Arthur and the knights of the Round Table. Finds of pottery, as well as early coins and two pillars inscribed during Roman times, suggest activity on the headland in the third and fourth centuries AD. Between 450–650AD, Tintagel was considered a rich and important site with much trade being carried out with the Mediterranean world. By the seventh century, the headland was abandoned and stayed like this for 500 years. In 1136 Geoffrey of Monmouth wrote his fictitious account of British History *Historia Regum Britanniae*. His legendary King Arthur was conceived at Tintagel by Uther Pendragon and Igerna, wife of Duke Gorlois of Cornwall. It wasn't, however, until between 1225 and 1233 that the castle on the headland was built by Richard, the Earl of Cornwall, who was Henry III's brother.

In 1337, the Black Prince, Edward, 1st Duke of Cornwall, reworked the castle's great hall into smaller buildings after erosion caused a partial collapse. In 1480, antiquary William Worcestre named Tintagel as the place where King Arthur was born and the legend grew.

King Arthur's Castle, Tintagel in the 1950s. In 1480, antiquary William Worcestre named Tintagel as the place where King Arthur was born and the legend grew.

By 1650 the legend of King Arthur had become a mixture of folklore and literary legend.

During Norman times, a small castle was built at Bossiney, before the Domesday Survey of 1086. In 1253 both Bossiney and Trevena were established as a borough by Richard, the 1st Earl of Cornwall. The Domesday Book mentions two manors in the parish. These were Bossiney, which was kept from the monks at Bodmin by the Earl of Cornwall. There was land for six ploughs and 30 acres of pasture. The monks at Bodmin held Treknow and there was land for eight ploughs and 100 acres of pasture.

The Duchy of Cornwall held seventeen Antiqua maneria (ancient manors) and Tintagel was one of these.

The parish feast is celebrated annually at Tintagel on 19 October, which is the feast day of St Denys, the patron of the chapel at Trevena. The market hall and the location of the fair were close to the chapel.

In 1552, the borough of Bossiney was granted the right to send two MPs to Parliament. It continued to do this until 1832 when its status as a borough was abolished. Until the early twentieth century, the nearby villages of Trevena and Bossiney were parted by fields by Bossiney Road.

Between 1840 and 1841 the Tithe Commissioners' survey took place and recorded that the overall area of the parish was 4,280 acres. Approximately 3,200 acres was arable and pasture land. Lord Wharncliffe, the largest landowner, owned 1,814 acres with 125 acres of glebe land.

Tintagel was formerly known as Trevena until the Post Office began using the name 'Tintagel' in the mid-nineteenth century. The village also has the 'Old Post Office', a building which dates from the fourteenth century. It became a post office during the nineteenth century and is now listed as a Grade I building which, today, is owned by the National Trust.

In the 1930s, major excavations were carried out by C.A. Ralegh Radford on and near the site of the twelfth-century castle. This revealed that the headland at Tintagel was once the site of an important Celtic monastery or a princely fortress and trading settlement dating from the fifth and sixth centuries. This period followed immediately

The Old Post Office at Tintagel. The building dates from the fourteenth century. It became a post office during the nineteenth century and is now listed as a Grade I building which, today, is owned by the National Trust.

after the withdrawal of the Romans from Britain. Finds included Mediterranean oil and wine jars which showed that sub-Roman Britain was not an isolated outpost as had previously been thought.

The area attracts thousands of visitors every year, many drawn by the area's supposed connection to King Arthur.

Boscastle lies 14 miles south of Bude and 5 miles north-east of Tintagel. The village's name comes from Botreaux Castle, which was a twelfth-century motte-and-bailey fortress. The castle originally belonged to the de Botreaux family.

In the mid sixteenth century, John Leland described the village as, 'a very filthy town and ill kept'.

The harbour has a natural inlet which is protected by two stone harbour walls. These were built by Sir Richard Grenville in 1584. The village was originally just a small port and imported limestone and coal as well as exporting slate and other local produce.

The harbour at Boscastle. The harbour has a natural inlet which is protected by two stone harbour walls. These were built by Sir Richard Grenville in 1584.

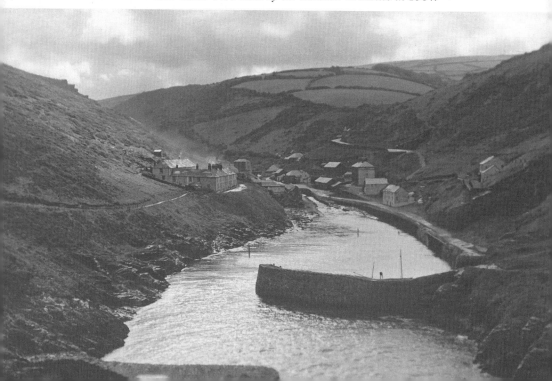

An early photo showing Fore Street in Boscastle. The village name comes from Botreaux Castle, which was a twelfth-century motte-and-bailey fortress.

Today it is popular with tourists and lies within the Cornwall Area of Outstanding Natural Beauty.

Bude is a seaside resort which lies south-west of Stratton. During the Middle Ages there was only one dwelling in the area which was Efford Manor, the seat of the Arundells of Trerice. It had a chapel of St Leonard. There was another chapel at Chapel Rock at the time, which was dedicated to Holy Trinity and St Michael.

During the eighteenth century, there was a small harbour at Bude but it was tidal which caused problems when the sea rose. The Bude Canal Company constructed a canal and strengthened the harbour.

River boating from Nanny Moore's Bridge, Bude in the early 1960s. During the Middle Ages, there was only one dwelling in the area which was Efford Manor. This was the seat of the Arundells of Trerice.

The canal's original purpose was to deliver mineral-rich sand from the beaches at Bude and take them inland to fertilise the fields. The enterprise suffered financial difficulty but managed to carry large volumes of sand as well as coal from south Wales. When the railway arrived at Holsworthy, together with the production of cheap manufactured fertiliser, the canal lost much of its use. It was eventually shut and was sold to the district municipal water company. The wharf and harbour had longer success, and coastal sailing ships delivered grain to Wales and brought coal back to Cornwall.

The Bude Lifeboat capsized when its steering oar broke on 10 October 1844. Two of the crew members drowned.

Until the beginning of the twentieth century, the neighbouring town of Stratton was dominant but Bude grew steadily over the following years.

Bude became a popular holiday destination for the middle classes in the latter part of Queen Victoria's reign. Sea bathing became popular as did sightseeing.

To facilitate this, the railway line was extended to Bude in 1898 which brought many tourists although it couldn't rival Newquay or other popular resorts in south Cornwall and Devon. Bude continues to be a popular destination for holidaymakers.

Cornwall today is renowned for its tourism which brings in much of the county's prosperity. Its history and beauty proves a great attraction and in many ways make it one of the most unique and interesting counties in the British Isles.

Acknowledgements

Most photos used in this book come from the author's personal collection. Special thanks go to Tina Cole and Tilly Barker. Tilly's investigation of historical sites of interest proved particularly helpful.

Bibliography

A History Of Cornwall by F.E. Halliday (House of Stratus, 2008)

Cornish Mines: St Just to Redruth by Barry Gamble (Alison Hodge, 2011)

Cornwall: A History by Philip Payton (Cornwall Editions Limited, 2004)

Cornwall at War by Derek Tait (Pen and Sword, 2017)

Cornwall Past and Present by Tom Bowden (Sutton Publishing, 1999)

Cornwall's History: An Introduction by Philip Payton (Tor Mark Press, 2002)

Cornwall's Secret Coast by Robin Jones (PiXZ, 2014)

Cornwall Through Time by Derek Tait (Amberley, 2012)

Lonely Planet Devon & Cornwall by Lonely Planet and Oliver Berry (Lonely Planet, 2014)

Lost Cornwall: Cornwall's Lost Heritage (Birlinn, 2016)

Mount Edgcumbe by Derek Tait (Driftwood Coast, 2009)

National Trust Histories: Cornwall by Jack Ravensdale (Retro Classics, 2015)

Rame Peninsula by Derek Tait (Amberley, 2010)

River Tamar Through Time by Derek Tait (Amberley, 2011)

River Tamar Through the Year (Amberley, 2012)

Saltash by Derek Tait (Driftwood Coast, 2008)

Saltash Through Time by Derek Tait (Amberley, 2010)

Smuggling in Cornwall: An Illustrated History by Jeremy Rowett Johns (Amberley Publishing, 2016)

The Little Book of Cornwall by John van Der Kiste (History Press, 2013)

The Maritime History of Cornwall: an Introduction by Helen Doe (Tor Mark Press, 2010)

Index